Growing Out: From Disciples To Disciplers

GROWING IN JESUS

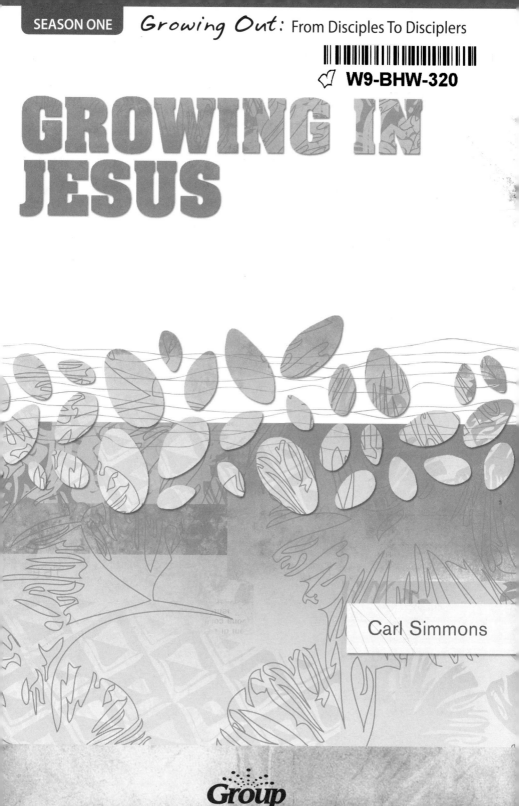

Carl Simmons

Group

Loveland, Colorado

group.com

Group resources actually work!

This Group resource incorporates our R.E.A.L. approach to ministry. It reinforces a growing friendship with Jesus, encourages long-term learning, and results in life transformation, because it's

Relational
Learner-to-learner interaction enhances learning and builds Christian friendships.

Experiential
What learners experience through discussion and action sticks with them up to 9 times longer than what they simply hear or read.

Applicable
The aim of Christian education is to equip learners to be both hearers and doers of God's Word.

Learner-based
Learners understand and retain more when the learning process takes into consideration how they learn best.

SEASON ONE

Growing Out: From Disciples To Disciplers

GROWING IN JESUS

Visit our website: **group.com**

Credits
Senior Editor: Candace McMahan
Executive Editor: Rebecca L. Manni
Chief Creative Officer: Joani Schultz
Copy Editor: Nancy Friscia
Art Director: Paul Povolni

Cover Designer: Holly Voget
Book Designer: Jean Bruns
Illustrator: Wes Comer
Print Production: Paragon Prepress
Production Manager: Peggy Naylor

Unless otherwise indicated, all Scripture quotations are taken from the *Holy Bible,* New Living Translation, copyright © 1996, 2004. Used by permission of Tyndale House Publishers, Inc., Carol Stream, Illinois 60188. All rights reserved.

ISBN 978-0-7644-3899-8

10 9 8 7 6 5 4 3 2 1   19 18 17 16 15 14 13 12 11 10

Printed in the United States of America.

Contents

What *Growing Out* Looks Like

Growing Out is more than a series of Bible studies—it's a progression that will take you and your group from becoming disciples of Jesus to becoming discipl*ers* of *others* in Jesus. As you move through each season, you'll grow from the inside out—and as you grow, your life in Jesus will naturally expand and branch out to others in your world.

And here's the best part: As you grow out together, you'll realize how much you're *already* discipling others—starting with those in your group!

Growing Out is designed to allow you to jump in at the most appropriate place for you and your group. To help you discover your entry point, take a look at these descriptions of each season:

Season 1: Growing in Jesus focuses on developing your relationship with Jesus. Because, let's face it, the first person you have to disciple is *yourself.* More to the point, you need to learn how to let Jesus *show* you how to be his disciple. So in this season, we focus on your relationship with Jesus and how to deepen it through spiritual disciplines such as prayer, worship, Bible study…and, not least of all, through your relationships with other Christians (such as the ones you're sitting with).

After you've been grounded in your relationship with Jesus, how does that shine into the rest of your life? That's where *Season 2: Growing in Character* comes in. This season focuses on how you can invite Jesus into your most important relationships—with your family, your friends, and the people you work with—and how to keep Jesus at the center of all of them.

Season 3: Growing in Your Gifts focuses on discovering the gifts, talents, and passions God has given you and how God might want to use them to serve others—whether that's inside or outside your church walls. After this season, you'll have a better sense of who God has created you to be, and why.

And with that, you're ready for *Season 4: Growing Others.* If you've gotten this far, you've developed and deepened your walk with Jesus, you've learned how to actually live it out among those people you most care about, and you've begun to discover how God has uniquely built you. Now…how do you take what God has shown you and help *others* walk through the same process?

If you've completed Seasons 1 through 3, you already know the answer because that's *exactly* what you've been doing with your group. Season 4 will help you reach out to even more people. Call it mentoring, discipling, or just being a good Christian friend to someone who needs it, after Season 4 you'll be ready to come alongside anyone who's ready to have a deeper relationship with Jesus. Just as you were in Season 1.

In the final two seasons, you'll explore what it takes to lead others where God wants you *and* them to go next. Because as you've walked through the first four seasons, guess what? You've been growing. Others know it. And God is honoring it. So whether you see yourself that way or not, God has matured you to the point where you're ready to lead. And we're going to help you get *more* ready.

Season 5: Growing in Leadership focuses on how to stay functional even as you learn how to lead. You'll walk together through the challenges of leadership—communication, conflict resolution, building consensus, learning how to adjust your ministry, and learning to stay focused on God instead of "*your* ministry."

And as you keep growing out, God may well put things on your heart that you'll need to be the one to initiate. That brings us, at last, to *Season 6: Growing in Your Mission.* God has given you a specific vision for ministry, and now you literally need to make the dream real. We'll help walk you through the issues that come with a God-given vision. Things like, first of all, how do you know it really *is* God and not just you? How do you get others on board (and praying—a *lot*)? And how will *you* keep growing, even as the vision continues to grow and take shape?

Because, no matter where you are, you never stop *Growing Out.* God will always see to that.

Enjoy *Growing Out,* and may God bless you as you grow out together!

Why R.E.A.L. Discipleship Works

Before we go any further, go back and take one more look at the copyright page of this book (it's page 2—the one with all the credits). Go to the top of the page where it declares, "Group resources actually work!" Take a minute or two to read that entire section describing Group's R.E.A.L. guarantee, and then come back to this introduction. I'll wait for you here…

Now that we're literally back on the same page, let's explore R.E.A.L. a little more deeply. Your desire to go deeper is the reason you're reading this book, and it's not only our goal but also our *passion* to help you accomplish that desire. When it comes right down to it, there's nothing more R.E.A.L. than discipleship. Think about it:

Relational

At the heart of it, discipleship *is* relationship. First and foremost, it's about developing the most important relationship you'll ever have—your relationship with Jesus. And as your relationship with Jesus grows, it becomes far more than anything you've ever imagined.

Like any great relationship, it doesn't develop on its own. It's intentional. It's work. But it's way more than that. What we get back is far more than what we put in. How could it *not* be? It's a relationship with *Jesus.* And as that relationship grows, we'll want to bring Jesus into every other relationship we have.

So we've kept that in mind as we've designed these sessions. You'll gain a deeper understanding of God's Word, but even more important, you'll discover how to share what you've learned with those around you. And that discovery *has* to happen in community. We've made these sessions very relational because, after all, you're learning how to become disciplers. By definition, that means learning how to speak God into others' lives. As you do that, you'll get as much back as you give, if not more. Because that's what happens in great relationships.

You'll notice that we often suggest getting into pairs or smaller groups. That's because participation—and learning, not to mention life change—increases when everyone's involved. It's more challenging, sure, but it's also more rewarding. Be sure to take advantage of the times we suggest it.

All this is a long way of saying that by the time you've finished this season, not only will you have a deeper relationship with Jesus, but your spiritual relationships with others will be richer and deeper than you had ever anticipated. And when that happens, be sure to thank us; a little affirmation goes a long way toward helping us to keep doing what we do here.

Experiential

Experiences? Yeah, we've got experiences. And as you discover together where God wants to take you next, you'll have experiences of your own long after you've completed these sessions.

Research has proven again and again that the more senses we engage in the learning process, the more likely a session is to stick and truly become woven into our daily lives. Jesus knew that, too. That's why he used everyday items to make his message more real. Not only that, but he invited people out of their comfort zones to conquer their fear of the unknown. We like to do that, too. A lot.

And because it's so different from what we're used to when studying God's Word, this is often the hardest part of R.E.A.L. learning for people to embrace. Is it *really* OK to have fun when we're studying the Bible? Does it truly honor God? Wouldn't it distract us from focusing on God?

First, let's make it clear that these are legitimate concerns. I've wrestled with all of them as I've developed these sessions.

We want to honor Jesus. Discipleship isn't a joke. It's serious business. It's about the rest of your life and how you'll glorify God with it. There's nothing more serious than that.

Nonetheless, sometimes the best way to get serious is to set aside our expectations first, so we're able to open up and get down to what we're *really* wrestling with, rather than just come up with the right answers, go home, and never really deal with the things God wants us to deal with. The experiences in this book go a long way toward accomplishing that. Here are just a few of the ways people "got R.E.A.L." as we field-tested this curriculum:

- A church elder in our group declared from the beginning, in no uncertain terms and with a bit of a growl, "I don't *do* games." A few weeks in, he shared, "This is exactly what [my wife and I] needed right now." Several weeks later, this same game-hating elder proclaimed, "I really *liked* that activity! It worked *perfectly!*"

- One of our hosts, who also prepared the session's snack, suggested, "I'll make sure I pull it out of the oven just when everyone gets here." She understood that not only the look and taste of the snack but also the smell would help people experience the session more acutely.

- A pastor in our group enjoyed one particular activity so much that he went ahead and used it in his own church's small-group training class.

- Another woman shared how her husband had been initially skeptical about R.E.A.L. learning and about small groups in general. (Anyone else detecting a pattern among the men, by the way?) Several sessions later, she was positively glowing as she shared how we'd "broken through" and how much he'd opened up as we'd gone along—and for that matter, how he was still talking about the session the next morning.

Discipleship *is* a lifelong adventure. And we're here to help you embrace that adventure. Together. That's why we've not only built in activities to get you thinking about your faith (and expressing it) in brand-new ways, but...well, let's just move on to...

Applicable

This is pretty straightforward. You're here not only to learn but also to grow. And that means taking what you've learned and using it.

We give you opportunities in every session to do that—to give you a safe place to experiment, if you will. We also provide opportunities at the end of each session for you to take what you've learned and "Walk It Out" in the rest of your life—so that your faith *becomes* your life, and you can take practical steps toward sharing your life in Jesus so others can see and respond to it as well.

Learner-Based

For some of you, the Bible passages and ideas you're studying may be familiar. But as you explore them in fresh ways in these sessions, you'll experience and understand God's Word in ways you've never considered before. We're studying God's living Word, after all. So we want to help you not only learn brand-new things but also find new significance and meaning in familiar and taken-for-granted ideas.

Therefore, we've been very deliberate about choosing the right approaches for the right sessions. When an activity works, let's get up and do it. If a movie clip brings out the meaning of what you're learning, throw in the DVD and let's talk. If a snack not only works as an icebreaker but also as a discussion starter about a much deeper subject, let's serve it up and dig in. And when it's time to just open up God's Word and really wrap our minds around what God wants us to understand about a given subject—or to be reminded of what God has already shown us (because we forget that all too easily, too)—then we'll bust out our Bibles and read as many passages as it takes to begin to grasp (or re-grasp) that.

You're also here to discover who *you* are in Jesus. The body of Christ is made of millions of unique parts. You're one of them. We *know* one size doesn't fit all, and we've built *Growing Out* to reflect that. So whatever reaches you best—the Bible study, the activities, the questions, the take-home pieces, whatever—use them to their fullest extent. I'll give you some more ideas of how to do this in the next two sections.

However you approach these sessions—and whether you do that as a leader or as a participant—be sure to help others in your group approach things in the ways God can best reach them. And as God works in all of you, celebrate it. A lot.

May God bless you as you begin your journey together. And as God takes each of you to the places and experiences he has prepared for you, never forget: You're all in this together. You, God, and everyone he puts in your path. And *that's* discipleship.

—*Carl Simmons*

About the Sessions

Now that you know why we do what we do, let's talk about *how* we do it—and more important—how *you* can do it.

You may already understand this, but just so we're clear: Discipleship is *not* about completing a curriculum. It's about developing and deepening the most important spiritual relationships you have—first with God, then with those God brings you in contact with—because *none* of those relationships is an accident. They're all intentional, and we need to be intentional as well.

In fact, that's why we refer to each study as a season, rather than as a study, book, or quarter. We each grow at our own pace. Your season of growth might be longer or shorter than someone else's, and that's OK. God will take as long as you need to get you where he wants you. So spend as much time in each season as you need to. But stay committed to moving forward.

Also, each season has been built so that whether you're a participant or a leader, you can get the most out of each session. And that starts with the layout of each lesson. Keep a finger here, flip over to one of the sessions, and let's look at why this is so different.

This isn't just a leader guide. It's not just a guide for group members. It's *both!* And the way we've set up the sessions reflects that.

Leaders: The left-hand pages contain *your* instructions, so you're constantly on track and know what's happening next. What you do, what you say—all the basics are there. You'll also want to be sure to check out the "Leader Notes" beginning on page 189—they'll give you specific prep instructions for each session as well as great tips to make each session the best it can be.

Group Members: You don't care about all that leader stuff, do you? Didn't think so. Now you don't need to. The right-hand pages are just for you. Write your answers, journal whatever else God is saying to you, record insights from your group discussions, doodle while you listen—you've got plenty of room for all of it. All the questions and Bible passages you'll be using are right there. Use your pages to get the most out of what God is showing you each week.

Got all that? Good. Now let's talk about what each session looks like.

Come and See

In this (usually) brief opening section, you'll take time to unwind and transition from wherever you're coming from—a hectic drive to church on a Sunday morning or the end of a busy day—into the theme of the session. You and your group might enjoy a snack or a movie clip together; maybe it'll be an activity; maybe you'll just talk with someone else. Then you'll be ready to dig in deep. And maybe—because you were too busy having such a good time doing it—you won't even realize that you've already gotten down to business.

Seek and Find

This is the heart of each session and usually the longest section. You'll spend roughly a half-hour digging into God's Word and discovering its meaning in a way you hadn't realized before. You think you understand these things now? Just *wait*. Through a variety of experiences and powerful questions that take a fresh look both at Scripture and at what's going on in your own head and heart, you'll discover how God's Word *really* applies to your life.

Go

Now you'll move from understanding how what you've been studying applies to your life to considering ways to act on it. Again, through meaningful experiences and questions, you'll discover what you can do with what God has shown you through today's session. Which will take you directly into…

Walk It Out

This is the take-home part of the session. With a partner or partners, you'll each choose a weekly challenge to apply this session to your life in practical ways in the coming week and beyond.

We've broken out the challenges very specifically, to meet you wherever you are:

know it
Some of you are visual learners—you get it by reading it. Others of you just don't feel comfortable being "outward" in your faith yet. This section's for you. We'll give you ways to reflect on God's Word, internalize it, and ultimately start sharing it in ways you might not have considered before.

live it
This suggestion is usually for the more reflective among you. You want to share what God is doing, but you need to process what God is doing in *you* before you can share it with anyone else. The ideas here will help you do just that.

share it
You're already a relational person, and God built you that way. Therefore, you're ready to share Jesus with someone else in a meaningful way. So here's a way to do it. Now go make it happen!

go for it
You're probably a more creative or kinesthetic type. You want to share your faith, but you also want to do something a little more out-of-the-box. We've got just the thing for you. And here's where you'll find it.

do it together
Here are suggestions for something you can do together as a group. It might be an outreach event, a retreat, or just a great get-together outside your session time. Every so often, try one of these as a group, and see what God does with it.

By the way, if God has really spoken to you about something else during a session and you know you need to do whatever he's urging you to do, don't feel you have to choose from the ideas we've provided. Be obedient. Share what God is showing you with your group so they can pray for you and encourage you.

There's one more section to tell you about. It appears at the very end. It's not even part of the session per se, but it could end up meaning a lot to you.

Go Deeper I can't emphasize this enough,
so I'm repeating it: Discipleship is *not* about completing a curriculum. It's about developing and deepening the most important spiritual relationships you have—first with God, then with those God has brought you in contact with— because *none* of those relationships is an accident.

Therefore, it's possible you'll work through this season and think, Before I go any further, I *really* need a deeper understanding of... That's why we've provided a list of resources at the end of each session to help you do just that. At Group, we're not shy about recommending other publishers—and if a resource applies to more than one area of spiritual growth, we'll recommend it more than once. This isn't about selling Group products (although there's always much more dancing in the halls here when that happens). It's about your growing relationship with Jesus and about being willing to invite God into whatever you're still wrestling with.

And that painful thing you're feeling when you do that? That's called growth. But the good news is that we're in this together. So pull over whenever you need to! Or jump right into the next season. We're here for you either way.

Which brings us to a little reminder: If there's an area in which you'd like to see *us* dig deeper and create more resources to help *you,* tell us! Write to us at Group Publishing, Inc., P.O. Box 481, Loveland, CO 80539; or contact us via e-mail at smallgroupministry.com. We'd love to hear what you're thinking. (Yes—*really!*)

Choose Your Environment

Growing Out works well in a variety of venues. We want to help you wherever you are. Don't be shy about trying any of them! Here are some additional ideas, depending on your venue.

Sunday School

First, you may have noticed that I've chosen the word *group* instead of *class* throughout. Not every group is a class, but every class is a group. You're not here just to study and learn facts—you're also here to learn how to live out what you've learned. Together. As a group. We hope that becomes even truer as you work through these sessions.

We've constructed these sessions to run an hour at a brisk pace, but we understand the limitations a Sunday school program can put on the amount of time you spend on a session. So if a great question has started a great discussion and you don't want to cut it off, feel free to trim back elsewhere as needed. For example, since much of our field test group was made up of couples who could talk on the way home, we discovered that making "Walk It Out" a take-home instead of an in-class piece was one good way to buy back time without losing impact.

Try not to be one of those groups that say, "Great—we can skip that experience now!" Remember, the more senses and learning styles you engage, the more these sessions will stick. So play with these activities. Give yourself permission to fail—but go in expecting God to do the unexpected.

And if you don't have specific time limitations, read on.

Small Groups

If you need more than an hour for a session—and you're not tied to a clock or a calendar—take it! Again, taking the time to understand what God wants to tell your group is *way* more important than "covering the material" or staying within the one-hour or 13-week parameters. This happened repeatedly while field-testing—a great discussion ensued, people got down to things they were really wrestling with, and we decided we'd explore the session further the following week.

Learn to recognize rabbit trails—and get off them sooner rather than later—but don't short-circuit those occasions when the Holy Spirit is really working in people's lives. Those occasions will happen often in these sessions. If you're having a rich discussion and are really digging in, take an extra week and dig even deeper. Give the full meaning of the session time to sink in.

One-on-One Discipleship

Although this curriculum is designed for a larger group setting, we absolutely don't want to discourage you from using it in a more traditional, one-on-one discipleship setting. True, some of the activities might not work in a setting this small, and if that's the case, feel free to bypass them and go directly into the Bible passages and questions— there are plenty left to work with. The important thing is that you work together through the issues themselves, and at the pace that works for you.

But don't take this as an opportunity to entirely excuse yourselves from experiences—have a little fun together, and see what God does. Allow yourselves to be surprised.

Also—and it's probably obvious for this and the next scenario—all those recommendations we make to form smaller groups or twosomes? You can skip those and jump right into the discussion or activity.

Smaller Groups or Accountability Groups

One more thing: We don't want to discourage you from doing one-on-one discipleship, especially if you've already got a good thing going. There are some great and healthy mentoring relationships out there, and if you're already involved in one, keep at it! That said, research has shown repeatedly that learning can happen at a more accelerated rate—and more profoundly—in settings other than the traditional teacher-student relationship. So if you're just starting out, consider gathering in groups of three or four.

- A small group provides an environment that allows people to learn from one another. While there's often still a clear leader, the playing field feels more level, and the conversations often become more open and honest.

- If one person leaves for any reason—and there are plenty of legitimate ones—the group or accountability relationship isn't finished. Everyone else presses forward. No one is left hanging.

- The dynamics of a group of three or four are simpler than those of larger groups. And a group of three or four can be the best of both worlds, offering the rich discussions of a large group and the intimacy and accountability of one-on-one relationships.

- Again, we're about creating disciplers, and a smaller group allows growing disciplers to test-drive their own instructions, struggles, and transparency in an environment in which they can be both honestly critiqued and whole-heartedly encouraged. And when that happens, growth happens—for everyone.

If you'd like to delve into this further, Greg Ogden's *Transforming Discipleship* (InterVarsity) is a great resource to get you started, as are any number of materials from ChurchSmart Resources (churchsmart.com).

Whatever setting or environment you use for *Growing Out,* use it to its fullest. May God bless your efforts and those of the people with whom you share life!

Getting Connected

Pass your books around the room, and have people write their names, phone numbers, e-mail addresses, and birthdays in the spaces provided. Then make it a point to stay in touch during the week.

name	phone	e-mail	birthday

How Did We Get Here, and Where Are We Going?

So all of us who have had that veil removed can see and reflect the glory of the Lord. And the Lord—who is the Spirit—makes us more and more like him as we are changed into his glorious image" (2 CORINTHIANS 3:18).

In this session, we'll journey...

from ─────────────→ **to**
examining where we already are in our relationships with Jesus...

helping others see what that relationship means to us—and can mean to them.

Before gathering, make sure you have...

○ paper, cut into quarter-page slips—enough for everyone

○ pens or pencils for everyone

Come and See

(about 10 minutes)

LEADERS:

Please note that the bolded sections of text are for you to read aloud. Feel free to change the wording to make yourself more comfortable. Or just use ours; that's why it's here.

Pass your books around the room, and have each person write his or her name, phone number, and e-mail address in the space provided on page 22. You can do this either at the beginning or end of your time together.

》 Form groups of four or five—try to get with others you'd like to know better rather than those you already know well. Introduce yourselves, and take a few moments to share what you're each hoping to get out of this season.

Allow two or three minutes for discussion, and then regain everyone's attention.

》 Staying in your groups, share with each other exactly how you traveled here today. Be specific—include turns, landmarks, or whatever the rest of your group would need to know to make the same trip.

Allow another two or three minutes for discussion, and then bring everyone back together. Discuss these questions:

》 Today we're going to look at how far we've already come with Jesus. We'll discuss where and how we first connected with Jesus and where he's taken us since then. We'll explore how that relationship can shine so others can see it more clearly. Then we'll take the next step in our journey together!

Come and See

◎ Who in your group had the toughest trip here? Why?

◎ What parts of everyone's directions in your group were similar or the same? Explain.

◎ What parallels could you draw between your travels here today and your individual walks with Jesus? What's totally different between the two?

Seek and Find

(about 25 minutes)

Have one or more volunteers read Acts 26:1-29, and then discuss these questions:

>> **Not everyone's story is as dramatic as Paul's, but all the elements of a good faith story are here, in Paul's. So let's use Paul's model to better understand how our relationships with Jesus have shaped and changed our own lives. Rejoin the groups you were with earlier, and discuss the following questions. (It's very easy to get excited about what Jesus has done for us, so keep your answers brief so that everyone has a chance to share.) We'll come back together in 15 minutes.**

Allow 15 minutes for groups to share, and then call everyone back together.

>> **Isn't it amazing to consider the difference Jesus has made in our lives?**

Normally we're not going to have a lot of homework during this season, but we will this week. Over the next week, spend some time writing down your answers to those last three questions in more detail—what your life was like before you really had a relationship with Jesus, how you've encountered Jesus, and how your life has been different because of it.

There are extra pages at the end of this session to write your thoughts. Keep your faith story to about three minutes—which comes out to about two handwritten pages or one typewritten page. Do your best to write your faith story in a way that reads like *your* story. We'll work on that a bit more next week, but come with at least a solid first draft.

So what else can we do to help others understand what Jesus has done for us—and what he can do for them? Let's consider in more depth how God has already spoken to us.

> "*I could tell you adventures beginning from this morning,' said Alice in* Alice in Wonderland, *'but it's no use going back to yesterday, because I was a different person then.' Christians all say they are different persons than they were before their conversion—and they are!*
> —Robert C. Shannon, One Thousand Windows

 **Acts 26:1–29**

◎ How would you describe Paul before he met Jesus?

◎ How was Paul changed by his encounter with Jesus, and how did Paul's transformation affect others?

◎ What was your life like before you knew Jesus? (Or, if you were raised to be a Christian, before your faith became personal to you?) What were *you* like?

◎ How did God finally get your attention? How did you respond?

◎ How has your life been different because you know Jesus? What spiritual landmarks in your life can you point to where you can confidently say, "I *know* Jesus was in that"?

Go

(about 20 minutes)

>> **Let's look at some other verses about making our faith in Jesus visible to others.**

Ask for volunteers to read the following verses aloud:

- Matthew 5:13-16
- Acts 2:46-47
- Philippians 2:12-15.
- Matthew 28:18-20
- 2 Corinthians 3:12-18

Then discuss: ———————————————————————

Give everyone a slip of paper, and make sure everyone has a pen or pencil.

>> **Jesus has revealed himself to each of us and wants to use us to share his love with others. We can share it verbally...we can model Jesus' love in practical ways...we can be so overwhelmed by Jesus that we simply radiate his joy...but it's a critical part of our own faith to allow what Jesus has done in our lives to be visible to others.**

On the slips of paper you've just received, write a favorite Bible verse or passage. Feel free to use your Bibles if you need help finding a favorite passage. If you can't think of one particular favorite, choose a verse that stood out to you today. If you don't know the passage by heart, that's OK—just write it in your own words. Use the full slip of paper to write it, if you can, but don't include the actual chapter and verse (for example, John 3:16). Don't let anyone see what you've written. When you've finished, take a few moments to reflect on why this Scripture has meaning for you and how God has used it to speak to you.

Matthew 5:13-16; Matthew 28:18-20; Acts 2:46-47; 2 Corinthians 3:12-18; Philippians 2:12-15

◎ How can we show our faith to others, according to these verses?

◎ What elements of faith-sharing are we responsible for? Which parts is God responsible for?

Go _continued_

These sessions include many active-learning experiences like the one you've just done. At first, these activities may seem unusual. But research has proven again and again that the more fully we engage in the learning process, the more likely a session is to stick and really become woven into our daily lives. And that's what we all want to happen, right?

So give it a shot. If you believe it will work, it will! Your willingness to lead and your enthusiasm will help others get out of their comfort zones and conquer their fear of the unknown. Discipleship is a lifelong adventure. Learn God's eternal truth in brand-new ways—and take some time to enjoy it, and each other, as you do!

Allow a minute or two for everyone to write and reflect; then ask everyone to rejoin their smaller groups one more time.

》 Tear your slip of paper into enough pieces so that everyone in your group will have a piece. Then give each person one piece of your favorite Bible verse. Give everyone in your group a chance to guess what verses they have pieces of—and if you have time, whose verses they are. Afterward, discuss these questions:

Allow 10 minutes for discussion, and then have everyone get into pairs and proceed to "Walk It Out."

◎ What was the verse you shared, and how has God spoken to you through it?

◎ How was this activity similar to how we show *some* parts of our faith to other people but not other parts?

◎ What parts of your faith do you allow to show, and what pieces do you keep hidden? What could you do to give others a more complete picture of what God has done in your life?

Walk It Out

(about 5 minutes)

》 The following options are here to help you put what you've learned into practice. But if God has prompted you to do something else through this session, then by all means do that!

---

choose 1:

☐ know it

Learn how others have been changed by their encounters with Jesus. Read Acts 22, and compare it to what you've already read in Acts 26. Or read 2 Peter 1:12-18. Ask Jesus to make those same kinds of changes in you and in the people your life touches.

☐ live it

Where have you encountered Jesus in the past? A mountaintop? Your kitchen? (Or, in my case, a gas station?) If possible, go there this week. Reflect on how knowing Jesus has changed your own life, and spend a significant chunk of time thanking him for it. Then share what you've experienced with someone.

☐ share it

Get together with a friend this week, and share what God has done in your life. You could share the faith story you're working on this week or how God helped you through a situation similar to one your friend is facing now. Do more than just talk, though—listen for opportunities to encourage and pray for your friend.

Form pairs, select the option you'd like to take on this week, and share your choice with your partner. Write what you plan to do in the space provided, and make plans to connect with your partner before the next session to check in and encourage each other. Take five minutes to do that now.

Come back together as a group. Thank God for all he's done in your life. Ask God to give you a deeper appreciation of it. Ask God to give you the ability to let your light shine before others.

ⓒprayer

Walk It Out

☐ go for it

Make a list of the people you see regularly. Think of ways you can reflect Christ's hope to one or two of them this week. Invite someone over for dinner. Fix a neighbor's broken lawn mower. Smile at the cashier in your grocery store and ask how he or she is doing. You could even… well, what's something you could do?

☐ do it together

As a group, show Jesus' love and hope through your actions. Plan a simple service project for your community. For example, hand out bottles of water in the park on a hot day, walk through your neighborhood and pick up trash, or offer your neighbors a window-washing service. And if people ask why you're doing it, tell them!

…or think of your own!

Because of what Jesus has done in my life, I'll "Walk It Out" by

_____

_____

_____

_____

My Faith Story

Go Deeper

For those wanting to dig deeper into understanding and communicating their walk with Jesus so far, here are some great resources:

God Space: Where Spiritual Conversations Happen Naturally by Doug Pollock (Group)

Just Walk Across the Room: Simple Steps Pointing People to Faith by Bill Hybels (Zondervan)

Experiencing God: Knowing and Doing the Will of God by Claude V. King & Henry T. Blackaby (B & H Publishing/Lifeway)

What ~~Would~~ *Did* Jesus Do?

This means that anyone who belongs to Christ has become a new person. The old life is gone; a new life has begun!" (2 CORINTHIANS 5:17)

In this session, we'll journey...

from ───────────────→ **to**

sharing how much we know
Jesus has already done for us...

understanding how God's
unchanging truth fits into our
own faith stories.

Before gathering, make sure you have...

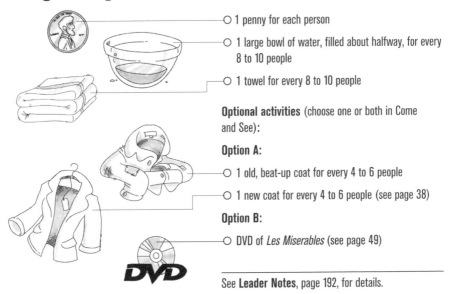

○ 1 penny for each person

○ 1 large bowl of water, filled about halfway, for every 8 to 10 people

○ 1 towel for every 8 to 10 people

Optional activities (choose one or both in Come and See):

Option A:

○ 1 old, beat-up coat for every 4 to 6 people

○ 1 new coat for every 4 to 6 people (see page 38)

Option B:

○ DVD of *Les Miserables* (see page 49)

See **Leader Notes**, page 192, for details.

37

Come and See

(about 15 minutes)

If you've chosen **Option A***, read on.*
If you're doing **Option B***, go to page 49.*

》 **Thanks for coming! I know you've just arrived and gotten comfortable, but I'm going to ask you to put on coats anyway—the coats you see over there.**

Ask people to gather into groups of four to six by each pair of coats.

》 **Everyone should try on the old coat first. But don't just put it on and take it off again—try to get comfortable in it. Take a whiff of it; get a feel for where this coat has been.**

> *Cleansing from sin and being made holy are not merely doctrines, they are acts of God, and experiences of the people of God. Neither doctrine can be taught without first being experienced, for the Christian is primarily a witness...who has personal knowledge of what he is talking about.*
>
> *—William H. Pape, The Lordship of Jesus Christ*

Put on one of the beat-up coats, and show everyone how it's done.

》 **Once you've done that, pass the old coat on to the next person to try on while you try on the new one. Again, leave it on for a few moments—get a feel for where this coat *hasn't* been yet and what kind of person might wear it.**

Pass on your beat-up coat to the next person, and repeat your actions with the new coat. Once everyone's had a chance to try on both coats, bring everyone back together and ask: ————

Ask for a volunteer to read Ephesians 4:22-24; then discuss these questions: ————

》 **A relationship with Jesus changes everything. Sometimes, though, we're still so wrapped up in how we see ourselves that it's hard to understand how deeply Jesus has already changed us—and how much deeper our relationship with Jesus can be.**

Today we're going to revisit our faith stories—how we've encountered Jesus so far, and how our lives have been different because of what Jesus has done for us. We're also going to look at what God's Word has to say about what Jesus has done for us, and see how much God's eternal truth is already true in our lives.

Come and See

 Ephesians 4:22-24

◎ How was trying on and taking off each coat like the taking off of the "old life" and the putting on of the "new life" that Paul describes here? How was it different?

◎ In what ways do you already know you're a new person in Jesus? What helps you see that?

◎ Which coat felt better? Explain.

◎ In what ways is it still tough to see yourself as a new person in Jesus? Why?

Seek and Find

(about 30 minutes)

》 **This past week you worked on your faith stories. Now you're going to find a partner and share that story.**

If you weren't here last week or haven't written anything down, briefly share what your life was like before Jesus, how you've encountered Jesus in your life, and how your life is different because of that. You'll each have five minutes to share your faith story.

Those of you listening: Wait until the other person has finished, and then take a couple of minutes to ask questions. Help your partner explain any parts of his or her faith story that aren't clear. Be curious. Also listen for instances in which God was clearly working in your partner's story. Point them out— especially if you don't think your partner has fully seen how present God was. Then switch roles.

Go ahead and partner up. We'll come back together in 15 minutes.

After seven or eight minutes, ask everyone to switch roles. After 15 minutes, call everyone back together, and then discuss these questions: ⎯⎯⎯⎯⎯⎯⎯⎯⎯⎯⎯⎯⎯

The world runs by ungrace. Everything depends on what I do...Jesus' kingdom calls us to another way, one that depends not on our performance but his own. We do not have to achieve but merely follow. He has already earned for us the costly victory of God's acceptance.

—Philip Yancey, What's So Amazing About Grace?

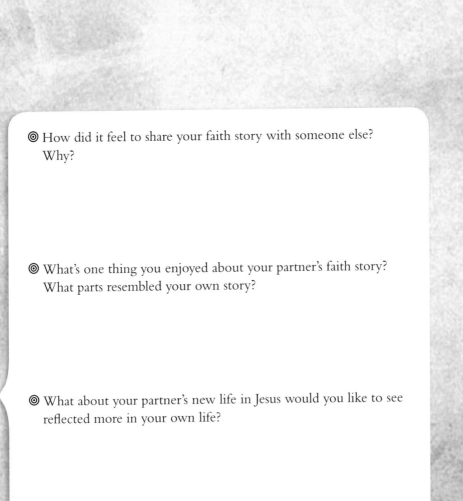

◎ How did it feel to share your faith story with someone else? Why?

◎ What's one thing you enjoyed about your partner's faith story? What parts resembled your own story?

◎ What about your partner's new life in Jesus would you like to see reflected more in your own life?

Seek and Find continued

》 **What we already know Jesus has done in our lives is amazing enough. But even more amazing is what God's Word says about what Jesus has done for us. Let's look deeper into Scripture and see for ourselves.**

Have everyone form groups of four or five.

》 **Divide the following list of verses among your group members. If someone needs to take two verses, that's OK. Read the verses to yourselves first, and write down in your own words what that passage says Jesus has done for you.**

When you've finished, share what you've written with the rest of the group. Then together, discuss these questions:

- John 15:13-16
- Romans 8:14-17
- 2 Corinthians 5:17-20
- Ephesians 1:11-14
- Ephesians 2:4-7

Come back together as a larger group, and share highlights and insights from your discussion.

✝ **John 15:13-16; Romans 8:14-17; 2 Corinthians 5:17-20; Ephesians 1:11-14; Ephesians 2:4-7**

◎ What encourages you about these verses? What intimidates you? Which ideas do you have trouble understanding?

◎ How might really understanding and believing what Jesus has done for you change the way you see yourself? the way you see others?

(about 10 minutes)

Stay together as a larger group. (If there are more than a dozen people, form groups of eight to 10.) Set the bowl(s) of water on a towel, and give everyone a penny.

》 One by one, close your eyes, make a wish, and toss your penny into the bowl of water. If you like, see how far away you can stand and still get the penny in the bowl!

After everyone has had a chance to toss a penny, discuss this question: —————————————————————————

Ask for a volunteer to read Ephesians 3:14-21. Then discuss these questions: ————————————————————————

◉ Be honest: For you, what's the difference between making a wish and tossing a penny, and talking to God in prayer? Explain.

✝ **Ephesians 3:14-21**

◉ When have you caught a glimpse into "how wide, how long, how high, and how deep [God's] love is"? How has seeing that affected your life? Be specific.

◉ Right now what (or who) could help you better understand—and remember—the width, length, height, and depth of Jesus' love for you?

Walk It Out

(about 5 minutes)

» **The following options are here to help you put what you've learned into practice. But if God has prompted you to do something else through this session, then by all means do that!**

GROUP ▼

choose 1:

☐ **know it** We've discussed huge ideas today. What does it really mean to be Jesus' friend? to be justified before God? to be adopted into God's family? Spend another hour meditating on this week's Scripture passages. As you encounter thoughts "too marvelous for words," stop right there and ask for God's help—God *does* know all things, and he wants to teach you. When you've finished, thank Jesus for all he's done, and ask him to help you know his love more and more.

☐ **live it** Set aside a specific time each day to talk to God. Tell God what's on your heart, and ask God to help you know what's on his heart. Who does God want you to reach out to? How does God want to stretch your faith? Don't limit your prayers to what you think you need. Ask God to show you what he *can* (and *wants to*) do in your life. The answers will probably surprise you.

☐ **share it** If you didn't do it last week, find someone outside of the group to share your faith story with. Be brave: Find a non-Christian friend, and tell him or her that you'd appreciate his or her help. Ask for your friend's feedback. What made sense? What didn't? Answer any questions, and if there are questions you can't answer, promise to find out and report back.

Form pairs, select the option you'd like to take on this week, and share your choice with your partner. Write what you plan to do in the space provided, and make plans to connect with your partner before the next session to check in and encourage each other. Take five minutes to do that now.

☐ **go for it** Who in your life is tough to love—someone you regularly exclude from your life? Do something to include that person. Invite him or her to lunch with you and a group of friends. Ask about his or her week, and *really listen* to the answer.

☐ **do it together**
As a group show Jesus' love in a concrete way to someone who needs it. Perhaps you can visit someone who's sick or shut in; maybe there's a home or car repair you can all do or help pay for. Think about how demonstrating this kind of love has affected how you feel about the people you're helping and about people in general.

...or think of your own!

Because of what Jesus has done in my life, I'll "Walk It Out" by

_____

_____

_____

_____

_____

Walk It Out _{continued}

Come back together as a group. Give everyone the opportunity to share one-sentence prayer requests. (Give people the option to pass if they choose not to share).

prayer⊙

Reread Ephesians 3:14-21, this time as a blessing for your entire group. Then pray for everyone's needs. Make sure that all the people in your group are prayed for, even if they don't have specific prayer requests. Thank God that our prayers to him are more than just wishes. Ask God to help all of you to truly "understand…how wide, how long, how high, and how deep his love is."

SEEING IT DIFFERENTLY
Come and See—Option B

LEADER *To prompt your group to think about a session in a fresh way, we'll occasionally recommend video clips that your group can enjoy in place of (or in addition to) another part of the session. You'll be surprised by how effectively movies can portray eternal truths, or at least point toward them.*

Instead of the coat activity, watch a scene from *Les Misérables* to experience Jesus' offer of a totally new life. Cue the movie to 0:06:05, when Jean Valjean is sneaking into the room to steal the bishop's silver. Stop the clip at 0:09:20, after he and the bishop finish their conversation in the garden. Then discuss the following questions:

GROUP

◎ In the face of what he'd done, how do you think Jean Valjean felt about the bishop's response to him?

◎ How do you think the bishop's actions affected Jean's life from that point on? Why?

Ask for a volunteer to read Ephesians 4:22-24, and resume the session with the question "In what ways do you already know you're a new person in Jesus?" on page 39.

Go Deeper

For those wanting to dig deeper into how their personal faith stories intersect with God's eternal truth, here are some great resources:

Just Like Jesus: Learning to Have a Heart Like His by Max Lucado (Thomas Nelson)

Group's BibleSense™: Ephesians: Seeing Ourselves in Jesus (Group)

Following Jesus: Biblical Reflections on Discipleship by N.T. Wright (Eerdmans)

Who Do You Love?

So why do you keep calling me 'Lord, Lord!' when you don't do what I say?" (LUKE 6:46).

In this session, we'll journey...

from ──────────────→ **to**
discovering what it really means
to follow Jesus...

trusting Jesus with every area
of our lives instead of just some.

Before gathering, make sure you have...

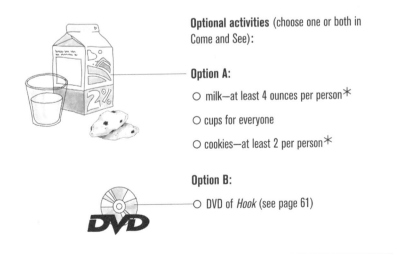

Optional activities (choose one or both in Come and See):

Option A:

○ milk—at least 4 ounces per person✳

○ cups for everyone

○ cookies—at least 2 per person✳

Option B:

○ DVD of *Hook* (see page 61)

─────────────────────

✳See **Leader Notes**, page 193, for details.

Come and See

(about 15 minutes)

If you've chosen **Option A**, *read on.*
If you're doing **Option B**, *go to page 61.*

» **Today we're going to start with a childhood snack—milk and cookies! Sorry, no naps afterward. So go get some milk and cookies, bring them back to your seat, and then we'll talk.**

While eating, discuss the following questions: ─────────

*Nondiscipleship
costs abiding peace,
a life penetrated
throughout by love...
hopefulness that
stands firm in the
most discouraging
of circumstances,
power to do what is
right and withstand
the forces of evil.
In short, non-
discipleship costs
you exactly that
abundance of life
Jesus said he came
to bring.*

—Dallas Willard,
The Great Omission

Ask for a volunteer to read 1 Corinthians 13:9-12, and then discuss: ────────────────────────────────

» **In some ways, it's good to be a child—Jesus himself told us to approach him as children, with a real sense of faith and expectancy, and we should seek to never lose that sense of childlikeness. On the other hand, many of us—including many who call ourselves Christians—are like the Lost Boys in *Peter Pan*. We never grow up, and as a result we never experience the kind of life Jesus came, and died, to give to us right here and now. Today we're going to try to grow up at least a little. We're going to take a harder look at what it costs to follow Jesus, and yet how much greater the rewards of following Jesus are.**

◎ What foods do you associate with your childhood?

◎ What memories do you associate with them?

✝ 1 Corinthians 13:9-12

◎ Is it always a bad thing to be like a child? Why or why not? In what ways do you feel like a child even now?

◎ On the other hand, where are you seeing God already starting to help you grow?

Seek and Find

(about 30 minutes)

>> Let's take one more look at what Jesus has already done in our lives. The more we realize what Jesus has done, the more we realize how much he still wants to do.

Form groups of four.

We need to lay before [God] what is in us, not what ought to be in us.

—C.S. Lewis

>> Read Philippians 3:12-17, and then discuss these questions: ——————————————

>> Come back together as a group, and share highlights from your discussion time.

In this passage from Philippians, Paul describes a race that we were meant to run for a lifetime. The good news is not only that God is calling us to reach the prize, but also that we have Jesus to coach us the entire way. With Jesus' help, we can reach the goal he has set before us.

Turn back one chapter in Philippians, and read chapter 2, verses 5-8.

Give everyone a minute to silently read Philippians 2:5-8.

>> I'm going to read the passage aloud a little differently, so you can listen for the connection between what Jesus has done and what God expects from us. I'll give you time to think and reflect. Time for you to connect with God. So relax and experience a time between just you and God. Simply listen. Close your eyes, and reflect quietly while I read.

Read the text on page 56 slowly and deliberately, pausing for at least 15 seconds where prompted:

✝ Philippians 3:12-17

◎ What's one area of your life in which you could honestly encourage others to "pattern your lives after mine" (verse 17)? (No false humility here—take time to be thankful for what Jesus has already done in your life.)

◎ How does dwelling on your past affect your ability to "reach the end of the race and receive the heavenly prize" (verse 14)? Can dwelling on your past ever be a good thing? If so, how?

◎ How would you describe "what lies ahead" for you right now? What do you think God is asking you to do to prepare for it?

Seek and Find continued

》 "You must have the same attitude that Christ Jesus had…
[who] did not think of equality with God as something to
cling to."

> In what ways do you still insist on doing things your
> own way instead of God's way? (Pause.)

"You must have the same attitude that Christ Jesus had…
[who] gave up his divine privileges."

> How have you allowed yourself to feel superior to
> others simply because you're a Christian? (Pause.)

"You must have the same attitude that Christ Jesus had…
[who] took the humble position of a slave."

> Who in particular have you refused to serve, whether
> by open rebellion or by quiet avoidance? Picture that
> person. (Pause.)

> When was the last time you claimed glory for yourself
> rather than giving it to God? (Pause.)

"You must have the same attitude that Christ Jesus had…
[who] humbled himself in obedience to God."

> What areas of your life have you not yet really submit-
> ted to God? What would it look like if you did? (Pause.)

"You must have the same attitude that Christ Jesus had…
[who] died a criminal's death on a cross."

> When do you still insist on defending your reputation,
> rather than trusting God and allowing him to defend
> you? (Pause.)

> *Frequently in
> our attempt to
> achieve Pentecost
> we bypass
> Calvary…Here
> is the spiritual
> principle: Die, and
> then bear fruit.*
>
> —Watchman
> Nee, The
> Messenger of
> the Cross

Now that we've taken the time to listen and reflect, return
to your groups of four. What did God show you during this
time of listening? Take time to talk—and listen—to one
another right now, and then close your time by praying
about the things God has shown each of you. We'll
regroup in 15 minutes.

Go

(about 10 minutes)

Call the entire group back together.

» Thank you for your openness and transparency with one another. By bringing our "stuff" out into the light, we're giving Jesus an opportunity to change us eternally. We're also giving others permission to keep us accountable and to support us as we continue to pursue God together, both inside and outside this class. I urge all of you to keep encouraging one another after we leave today.

We've given time to listening to God and one another; now it's time to talk about what's next. So we're going to spend a little extra time on prayer and commitment today. Let's form pairs and discuss the "Walk It Out!" options. Spend five minutes talking about your choices, and then we'll come back together to pray as a group.

Walk It Out

(about 5 minutes)

》 **The following options are here to help you put what you've learned into practice. But if God has prompted you to do something else through this session, then by all means do that!**

choose 1:

☐ know it

What did Jesus tell his own disciples about the cost of following him? Spend some time finding out this week. Read passages such as Matthew 4:18-22; 16:24-27; 21:28-32; Luke 6:46-49; 9:57-62; 10:1-24; and John 14:15, 24. Confess to Jesus those areas in which you haven't followed him; then ask him what changes you can make to follow him more closely right now.

☐ live it

Bury your past—literally. Do pain, trauma, or just plain bad decisions from your past still affect you today? Write them all down on paper, and ask God to give you the ability to let each of those things go. Then bury the paper(s) in the ground. Thank God for your past—because it has made you who you are today—but let it die so that your future can live.

☐ share it

Who can help you move forward in your faith? Find a mature Christian who'll encourage and challenge you. Choose someone who loves you enough to be honest with you—to tell you how you really are and to help you to become more Christ-like. Give this person permission to ask you personal questions about your life. Then act on his or her suggestions.

Form pairs, select the option you'd like to take on this week, and share your choice with your partner. Write what you plan to do in the space provided, and make plans to connect with your partner before the next session to check in and encourage each other. Take five minutes to do that now.

□ **go for it** Choose a thankless, undesirable act of service you can do this week. Scrub toilets, pick up trash in your neighborhood park, or baby-sit a neighbor's children (you know, the ones *no one* wants to be left alone with). Remind yourself of Jesus' amazing example of humility, and ask the Spirit to give you an extra portion of that humility as you take on this challenge.

□ **do it together**
Plan a service opportunity in which your group can show Jesus' love through caring for those living in meager circumstances. Serve a meal at a soup kitchen, or volunteer to work as a cleaning crew at a homeless shelter. At the end of your service time, read Philippians 2:5-8. What did Jesus teach you about the kind of love he has shown to us?

...or think of your own!

Because I want Jesus to be Lord of my entire life and not just parts of it, I'll "Walk It Out" by

_____

_____

_____

_____

Walk It Out continued

After five minutes, come back together as a group.

prayer⊙

》 Let's take a few minutes to pray silently about what God has shown us. Find something you have with you that represents what God has revealed to you today. For example, you could use a credit card to symbolize how God has pointed out your reliance on money or material things, or you could use your wedding ring to symbolize how you need to work on your relationship with your spouse.

Give everyone a few moments to locate a personal item.

》 Close your eyes and hold that item tightly in your fist. Hold on to it as tightly as you can. Silently ask for God's help. Ask God to show you how to rely on him first. Prayerfully trust God with that area of your life; then, as you do, open your fist and let your item drop.

Remain in an attitude of prayer until everyone has dropped his or her item, and then pray:

》 Father, we thank you that you want us to run the race well and that you are with us every step of the way. Please take these hurts, these disappointments, and all the other things that keep us from you. And as we give them over, replace them with your presence and your peace. In Jesus' name, amen.

SEEING IT DIFFERENTLY
Come and See—Option B

LEADER   Instead of (or better yet—while!) eating milk and cookies, watch a scene from the movie *Hook*. Cue the movie to 1:14:00 (DVD Chapter 15), in which Peter asks, "Eat what?" Stop the clip at 1:16:00, when Peter sits back down, and pick up at the reading of 1 Corinthians 13:9-12 on page 52.

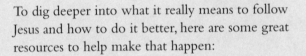

Go Deeper

To dig deeper into what it really means to follow Jesus and how to do it better, here are some great resources to help make that happen:

In Pursuit of Jesus: Stepping Off the Beaten Path by Rick and Bev Lawrence (Group)

What Jesus Demands From the World by John Piper (Crossway)

The Imitation of Christ by Thomas á Kempis (Moody, et al.)

The Cost of Discipleship by Dietrich Bonhoeffer (Touchstone, et al.)

The Spiritual Exercises of St. Ignatius of Loyola (ccel.org/ccel/ignatius/exercises, et al.)

Relationships Take Time

Then Jesus said, 'Let's go off by ourselves to a quiet place and rest awhile' " (MARK 6:31).

In this session, we'll journey...

from ⟶ **to**
examining the importance of a
regular quiet time...

discovering how we can deepen
our relationships with Jesus.

Before gathering, make sure you have...

○ a watch or clock with a second hand

See **Leader Notes**, page 193.

Come and See

(about 15 minutes)

》 **Thanks for coming! In the coming weeks, we'll be looking at different ways we draw closer to Jesus. Today we're going to focus on the importance of making time to just be with Jesus and how we can start giving priority to that time. Turn to a partner and share your responses to these questions:** ————————

> *True Christian experience must always include a genuine encounter with God. Without this, religion is but a shadow, a reflection of reality, a cheap copy of an original... The spiritual giants of old were men who at some time became acutely conscious of the real Presence of God.*
>
> —A.W. Tozer,
> The Pursuit of Man

》 **Jesus is our Lord and Savior—of course we're going to act a little differently around him! But Jesus also calls us his friends** (John 15:13-15), **and that's not something we should take lightly either. Jesus is the best friend we're ever going to have because he's going to be there for us, no matter what we're thinking or feeling, and he wants us to be there for him, too. If we're going to grow in a healthy relationship with Jesus, we're going to need to spend quality time with him. It's hard to love—let alone follow—someone you don't even know!**

Come and See

◎ Think about your best friend or about a best friend you had while growing up. Why is (or was) that person your best friend?

◎ What are some things you currently do to develop stronger friendships with others?

◎ OK, so what are some things you do (or can do) to develop a stronger friendship with Jesus? How are those things like or unlike how you approach your earthly friendships?

Seek and Find

(about 25 minutes)

》 **Let's spend some time discussing how we connect with Jesus. Form groups of three or four, and read Mark 6:30-32. Then share your answers to these questions:**

Allow 15 minutes for discussion, and then call everyone back together. Share highlights from your group discussions.

》 **It's not always easy to drop what we're doing so we can have refreshing times with Jesus. Some of us feel guilty about not giving our human obligations top priority. We may feel we're letting others down. A lot of us feel rushed and don't think we can get into "the right frame of mind" to "be" with Jesus. Some of us may even wonder whether we're wasting our time by doing what, humanly speaking, is...*nothing,* with Jesus.**

✝ **Mark 6:30-32**

◎ According to this passage, why did the disciples need to get away with Jesus? When have you thought of your own times with Jesus that way?

◎ Where or when do you tend to feel closest to Jesus? Why are those times or places more special?

◎ In general, when do you feel furthest from Jesus? Explain.

◎ Objectively speaking, do you really think Jesus is any closer to you or further away from you during the times you described? Why or why not?

Seek and Find continued

» **Let's take some time to be still with Jesus right now. In fact, we're going to be still for exactly 97 seconds. I'll keep an eye on the clock so I'll know when our time is up. Your job is to keep your eyes closed and to silently raise your hand when you think 97 seconds have passed. Keep your eyes closed until I tell you to open them. Ready?**

Begin now.

Wait about 15 seconds, remind everyone of the 97-second mark, and then introduce some "static" to everyone's quiet time by rambling on about anything that involves lots of numbers. Don't be obnoxious, but do be a distraction. Make sure people keep their eyes closed.

When all hands are raised, or after two minutes, ask everyone to open their eyes. Recognize the person or persons who came closest to raising their hands at the 97-second mark, and give them a round of applause. Then discuss these questions: —

All the unhappiness of men arises from one single fact, that they cannot stay quietly in their own room.

—*Blaise Pascal*

◎ How hard was it for you to be still for only a little more than a minute and a half? What kinds of things went through your mind during that time? Why?

◎ Why do we seem to be able to do everything except be still? What is it about quiet or stillness that makes us so uncomfortable?

(about 25 minutes)

Have people rejoin their groups of three or four. Ask them to read Luke 10:38-42 and Revelation 2:1-5, and then discuss these questions: —————————————————————————

Allow 10 minutes for discussion, and then call for everyone's attention. Have groups stay together, and ask them to share insights and highlights.

》》 Staying in your groups, I'd like you all to get quiet again, but this time we're going to focus directly on our relationships with Jesus. First, I'd like you to quietly reflect on the time you first drew close to Jesus. Starting now.

Allow 30 seconds of silence before saying anything further.

》》 Let's make sure we really capture the moment. Who was with you when that happened? Where were you? What were some of the sounds and smells? What were you thinking and feeling? Take another minute to replay that in your mind and heart. (Pause for one minute.)

Now quietly reflect on where you are right now in your relationship with Jesus. Think also about where you are in comparison to those first days, and why. (Pause.)

Now think about Jesus coming alongside you right now. What's different from before? What's better? And what do you miss from that first time you drew close to Jesus?

Allow 30 more seconds for everyone to reflect. Ask everyone to share their reflections in their groups. Then ask them to share their responses to this question: —————————————————————————

Allow five more minutes for discussion, and then ask groups to pair off and proceed to "Walk It Out."

† **Luke 10:38-42; Revelation 2:1-5**

◎ What's the connection between these two passages? What does Jesus approve of—and disapprove of?

◎ What are some ways we substitute "doing" for "being" in our Christianity? When can it be wrong to "do" good things—even good things for Jesus?

◎ What's one practical step you can take to make more time for Jesus?

Walk It Out

(about 5 minutes)

>> **The following options are here to help you put what you've learned into practice. But if God has prompted you to do something else through this session, then by all means do that!**

choose 1:

know it

Very few parts of the Bible say "time alone with God" like the Psalms. This week read as many as you can—all 150, if you're up for it; most are pretty short. If certain worship songs come to mind while reading, don't be embarrassed to sing them before God. Think about how you can incorporate the psalmists' attitudes into your own regular quiet time with God.

live it

Set aside a special quiet time for Jesus several times this week (every day, if you can). If you've never had a consistent quiet time, start with 15 minutes every morning. Bring God the things that have really been weighing on your heart lately. Spend time letting God's Word quietly speak to you. Or do…nothing. Just listen. The important thing is to come to God with an attitude of humility and expectancy. Let God do the rest.

share it

Ask God to do a "spiritual audit" on you and your relationships with others. One approach is to make SPACE for God: Is there a **S**in you need to confess? Is there a **P**romise you need to claim? Is there an **A**ttitude you need to change? Is there a **C**ommand you need to obey? Is there an **E**xample you need to imitate (or set)? Who do you need to approach, or what do you need to change, as a result of what God has shown you? Make it happen!

Form pairs, select the option you'd like to take on this week, and share your choice with your partner. Write what you plan to do in the space provided, and make plans to connect with your partner before the next session to check in and encourage each other. Take five minutes to do that now.

☐ **go for it** Who do you want to reach for God—in your family, your church, your work, your neighborhood, your community? Write all of your ideas down. Don't edit them yet—just put them on paper. When you've finished, present your list to God, and ask him to guide you into new and different ways to answer the needs you've written down. Invite someone from the group or a trusted friend to review your list with you. Then encourage and pray for each other.

☐ **do it together** As a group, hold a "listening day." Meet at your church or at a quiet, wooded park. Each person may bring a Bible, a devotional, a notebook, and a pen. Spend the first hour praying and worshipping together. Then have everyone go to a quiet place to be alone with God. Write down anything you believe God is saying to you. Finish up by sharing a meal together and talking about what you believe God has said to you.

...or think of your own!

Because Jesus deserves my time and attention, I'll "Walk It Out" by

_____

_____

_____

_____

Walk It Out continued

prayer⊙ Come back together as a group. Begin your prayer time together
with a few moments of silence. Then ask Jesus to help each person
find regular times to get away with him, and through those
moments to deepen each one's relationship with him.

Go Deeper

For those wanting to develop a deeper and more
fruitful quiet time, here are some great resources:

Come Away My Beloved by Frances J. Roberts
(Barbour)

Streams in the Desert by L.B. Cowman
(Zondervan)

*Invitation to Solitude and Silence: Experiencing God's
Transforming Presence* by Ruth Haley Barton
(InterVarsity)

*Hearing God: Developing a Conversational
Relationship With God* by Dallas Willard
(InterVarsity)

A Conversation With the Creator

So if you sinful people know how to give good gifts to your children, how much more will your heavenly Father give good gifts to those who ask him" (MATTHEW 7:11).

In this session, we'll journey...

from ——————————→ **to**
identifying our personal road-
blocks and false ideas about
prayer...

learning how to approach God
with a sense of expectancy.

Before gathering, make sure you have...

○ paper and pencils for everyone

○ enough tables and chairs for everyone to sit around

○ newsprint tablet, blackboard, or white board (If you're in a small-group setting, a notepad is OK.)

See **Leader Notes**, page 193.

Come and See

(about 15 minutes)

Distribute paper and pencils.

》 **I'd like us to start today's session by writing down our top priorities for today** [or tomorrow, if it's evening]. **It doesn't need to be a long list—five items will be plenty. Let's take a minute to write.**

Allow a minute for writing.

God: Every time I try to talk to someone, it's 'sorry this' and 'forgive me that' and 'I'm not worthy.'

—Monty Python and the Holy Grail

》 **Put your list in your pocket. You'll be glad you prioritized your day.** (Pause.) **Now turn to a partner and have a staring contest. Give him or her the blankest stare you've got. I'll let you know when it's OK to stop.**

Allow about 30 seconds for your staring contests.

》 **Find another partner, find a table to sit at if you're not already at a table, and have an arm-wrestling contest. It doesn't matter if one of you is significantly stronger than the other—but if you are, be gentle!**

Allow another 30 seconds, or until everyone has arm-wrestled at least once. One or more pairs might really get into their match—if so, allow them to finish; it'll make the point that much stronger later on.

》 **OK, one more thing: Turn to your current partner and say the first things that come into your head. They don't have to be deep or even make any sense—and you don't need to wait for your partner to stop talking—just say them. Go!**

Allow 30 more seconds for everyone to talk, and then get their attention. Ask everyone to remain in pairs.

》 **Congratulations! You've completed four very different tasks in a matter of minutes! Let's talk about them.**

Allow five minutes for discussion, and then call the group back together. Share highlights from your discussions.

》 We all know it's important to communicate with God in prayer. We know how important it is to engage our minds in prayer, to focus entirely on God, to be persistent and honest in our prayer, and to put everything we have on the table before God. But even with the best intentions, our prayers can sometimes feel mechanical, stupid, difficult, or as if we're just babbling.

You might be in a really good place in your prayer life right now. Maybe not. But we can always have a stronger, more intimate time with God in prayer. Let's look at some ways we can honestly, full-mindedly, and full-heartedly approach the Creator of the universe, who loves us and *wants* to answer our prayers.

▼ GROUP

◎ Which activity was most enjoyable? Why?

◎ Out of the four activities you did—the list-making, the blank staring, the arm-wrestling, and the talking off the top of your head—which one most resembles your prayer life right now? Or is your prayer life more like something else? Why?

◎ In terms of your prayer life, what can actually be good about each of these activities?

Seek and Find

(about 25 minutes)

Have everyone form groups of four, read James 5:13–18, and then discuss these questions:

> *Prayer does not fit us for the greater works; prayer is the greater work.*
> —Oswald Chambers, My Utmost for His Highest

Allow 15 minutes for discussion.

》 **Based on what you've shared, take 10 minutes to pray for one another in your groups. Start with a time of praise and thanksgiving. Thank God for who he is and how he's been there for you and the others in your group. Then join in those longtime prayers others in your group have been bringing to God. Share the burdens they've been carrying. Pray for encouragement for these people who have been faithfully taking these requests to God.**

After 10 more minutes, call the entire group back together.

✝ **James 5:13-18**

◎ When have you seen a direct answer to prayer, in your life or someone else's? Be specific. How were you changed by that?

◎ Now think about a time of personal (spiritual or emotional) drought in your life. What was it like? What ended that drought? How did you see God's faithfulness during (or despite) that time?

◎ What prayer or prayers have you been praying for a long time now? Have you ever felt like giving up on those prayers? What keeps you going?

Go

(about 15 minutes)

Ask for a volunteer to read Matthew 7:7-11, and then discuss the first two questions: ————————

As you discuss the third question, write down everyone's responses where all can see them, acknowledging each person's contribution as you do so. ————————

Then continue the discussion with the next two questions. ——

》 We started this session by writing down a list of priorities. I'd like you to pull that list out. Look it over. If there's something you forgot that really should be there, write it down now. We're going to take a few minutes to invite God into our [coming] day. Let's slow down here and *really* invite God in. Take your list and silently focus on giving each item to God.

Allow a few minutes for everyone to pray silently. Then have everyone find a partner and discuss this week's "Walk It Out" options. Let people know that once they've finished discussing and praying together, they're free to quietly leave (or quietly hang out until everyone's finished, if you're in a small-group setting).

✝ Matthew 7:7-11

◎ What do you think Jesus meant—and didn't mean—here?

◎ Think about a time you really prayed about something. What happened? How were your own thoughts and motives refined during that time?

◎ Why don't we always pray with the kind of expectancy Jesus describes here? List as many reasons as you can.

◎ Of all the reasons we just listed, which are the greatest obstacles to your own prayer life? Why?

◎ Think back to your prayer time from a few minutes ago. How can being thankful for what God has done in the past help you overcome these obstacles?

Walk It Out

(about 5 minutes)

》 **The following options are here to help you put what you've learned into practice. But if God has prompted you to do something else through this session, then by all means do that!**

GROUP ▾

choose 1:

☐ know it

Don't just read Scripture—pray it. Choose a favorite passage or use Psalm 23, Psalm 51, or John 17. Write the first verse, pause to reflect on its meaning, and then write a prayer based on how God speaks to you through that verse. Continue writing, reflecting, and praying until you've worked through the entire passage. Thank God for walking with you through his Word, and ask him for the wisdom to walk out your prayer in your daily life.

☐ live it

Whether or not you have a regular daily prayer time, switch things up this week. Each day, pray about one particular area of life. Here's one approach:

- Sunday: your church and its leadership
- Monday: your family
- Tuesday: your friends
- Wednesday: government leaders
- Thursday: your neighbors
- Friday: your co-workers
- Saturday: those with whom you've been sharing Jesus (or with whom you want the courage or opportunity to share Jesus)

Do whatever works, but do it all with a sense of expectancy that God is hearing and addressing your prayers.

☐ share it

Find a friend or co-worker who doesn't know Jesus but who you know needs prayer. Don't be shy about asking whether you can pray for—or better yet, with—that person. Even those who don't yet believe in Jesus are usually willing to take a chance on *your* faith. Give them the chance to do that this week.

Form pairs, select the option you'd like to take on this week, and share your choice with your partner. Write what you plan to do in the space provided, and make plans to connect with your partner before the next session to check in and encourage each other. Take five minutes to do that now.

☐ go for it Fasting

has profoundly affected many people's prayer lives. So give it a shot! If you're not used to fasting, start by abstaining from one meal, by fasting for half a day, or by fasting for 24 hours. Drink plenty of water to minimize your food-withdrawal symptoms. Use your mealtimes for prayer, discovering how God satisfies your needs in ways food never can. Consider giving the money you would have spent on food to an organization that works to eradicate hunger, such as World Vision, Compassion International, or Bread for the World.

☐ do it together

Sometimes the best way to discover the needs in your community is to get out there and look. So take a prayer walk around your community with your group. Pray for your neighborhood and the people you see in yards and houses; say hello to neighbors, and express an interest in their homes and lives. Ask for prayer requests so you can pray even more specifically. Consider prayer walking once a week for several weeks. Ask how neighbors are doing with the situations you've prayed about. This could build relationships that last a lifetime—and beyond.

...or think of your own!

Because I need to make prayer a more vital and basic part of my everyday life, I'll "Walk It Out" by

_____

_____

_____

Go Deeper

For those wanting to dig deeper into prayer, here are some great resources:

The Prayer Path: A Christ-Centered Labyrinth Experience (Group/Proost Publications)

With Christ in the School of Prayer by Andrew Murray (Wilder Publications; also known as *Teach Me to Pray*, Barbour)

Power Through Prayer by E.M. Bounds (Diggory Press)

Prayer: Finding the Heart's True Home by Richard Foster (HarperOne)

Praying Backwards: Transform Your Prayer Life by Beginning in Jesus' Name by Bryan Chapell (Baker)

Bible Study— Digging Deeper

Don't copy the behavior and customs of this world, but let God transform you into a new person by changing the way you think. Then you will learn to know God's will for you, which is good and pleasing and perfect" (ROMANS 12:2).

In this session, we'll journey...

from ⟶ **to**
exploring our need to know and study God's Word, and why we don't always do it... | discovering how the Bible can help our thoughts (and lives!) become more Christ-like.

Before gathering, make sure you have...

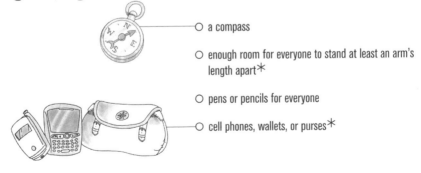

○ a compass

○ enough room for everyone to stand at least an arm's length apart ✳

○ pens or pencils for everyone

○ cell phones, wallets, or purses ✳

✳See **Leader Notes**, page 194, for details.

Come and See

(about 10 minutes)

Place the compass where everyone can see it but not read it.

>> **Everyone stand. Put at least an arm's length of space between you and the next person, preferably more. Also make sure you're at least an arm's length away from the nearest wall.**

Give everyone time to get into position.

>> **Now close your eyes...and point your arm straight ahead in the direction you think is north.** (Pause.) **Now, keeping your eyes closed, spin around three times. When you stop, point to the north again.**

Once all group members have stopped spinning and pointed in the direction they think is north, let them open their eyes. Chances are, arms will be pointed in very different directions.

Show the compass so everyone can see which direction is truly north. Then discuss these questions: ────────────

>> **God has given us a number of compasses to help us figure out what direction we should take, such as the guidance of the Holy Spirit and the advice of other mature Christians we trust. But sometimes we can mistake our own thoughts or feelings with what the Spirit is really trying to say to us. And even with the best of intentions, other Christians may give us advice that isn't what God wants for us.**

We have a compass that *always* points to God and can give us the guidance we need: the Bible. But many of us don't know how to use that compass to its best effect. Sometimes we don't believe it's really pointing north and don't follow it. Even more often, we don't pull it out to find out where God is trying to point us. And sometimes, we have a hard time reading that compass. But when we do use, understand, and follow God's Word, God changes us and takes us where he wants us. So let's see how we can make God's Word more a part of our lives and why it's important for us to do it.

" Because God knows the end from the beginning, not one of His statements ever turns out to be a misdirection. He does not shade the truth or leave out an essential part. His absolute truth applies to every situation."

—Bill Bright,
Discover God

Come and See

◎ What landmarks did you use to decide which way was north? How accurate were they?

◎ How accurate were you at pointing north *after* you'd finished spinning?

◎ When in your life have you felt as if you'd been spinning for so long that you didn't know which way was up (or north, for that matter)?

◎ What do you use as your "compass" when you have to make a tough decision?

Seek and Find

(about 35 minutes)

Have everyone form groups of four. Have them read the verses that follow, and then discuss these questions: ─────────

- Romans 12:1-2
- 2 Timothy 3:14-17
- Hebrews 4:12

- Psalm 1:2-3
- Psalm 119:105

Allow 15 minutes, and then call everyone together to share highlights and insights from your group discussions.

》 Now find Joshua 1:1-9 in your Bibles, and read the passage silently. Don't move on until you've read the whole passage. On your own, write your answers to these questions: ─────────

Give everyone five minutes to read and write individually.

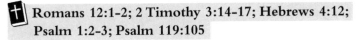

Seek and Find

✝ **Romans 12:1-2; 2 Timothy 3:14-17; Hebrews 4:12; Psalm 1:2-3; Psalm 119:105**

◎ What are the benefits of knowing God's Word, according to these passages? according to *you*?

◎ How have you seen some of these benefits in your own life?

✝ **Joshua 1:1-9**

◎ What's the context of this passage? In other words: What's happening here? When and where is this taking place? What do you think the people in the passage are thinking and feeling at this moment?

◎ What words or phrases in this passage stand out to you?

◎ What's the main thing God wanted the people in this passage to know?

◎ What's God saying to *you* through this passage? What's one way you can take what God is saying and put it into practice?

Seek and Find continued

》 Now return to your groups of four. Allow each person about a minute to share his or her answers. Then discuss these questions:

Allow 10 minutes for discussion, and then bring everyone back together.

》 At the end of this session is a section called "Tools of the Trade." It includes resources to help your study of God's Word become more meaningful, so on your own time review that section and consider what tools to add to your collection.

Let's move forward now.

> *Holy Scripture is more than a watchword. It is also more than 'light for today.' It is God's revealed Word for all men, for all times.*
> —*Dietrich Bonhoeffer, Life Together*

◎ Read Joshua 1:8-9 again. What's the difference between meditating on God's Word and just reading it?

◎ When (or how) has spending time in God's Word given you strength or success you wouldn't have had otherwise? Talk about it.

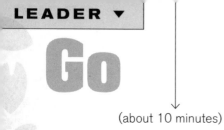

(about 10 minutes)

》 Take out your cell phone—or a wallet or purse if you don't have a cell phone—and put it in front of you.

Give everyone a few moments to get out their items. Then discuss:

》 We just looked at a passage in Scripture that commands us to meditate upon God's Word day and night. So let's take that idea a step further.

Let's try an experiment this week and make this idea more than just a nice activity we talk about. This week take your Bible everywhere you take the item you just pulled out.

Yes, *everywhere*.

It's likely you'll get some interesting looks from people; you'll almost certainly get a few questions. But who knows? You just might get the opportunity to share your faith with someone whose curiosity has been piqued. And as an added bonus, whenever you have the urge to read your Bible, it'll be right there. And because it's right there, you'll probably have that urge more often than you would have otherwise. So take a chance this week, and give God an extra opportunity to speak to you through his Word.

◎ What's so important about carrying this
thing with you everywhere you go?
What are some different ways you use it?

◎ What do you think would happen if your Bibles were as "joined to your
hip" as your cell phones, wallets, or purses are?

◎ How would giving God's Word time and priority in your life change
how you live? Be specific.

Walk It Out

(about 5 minutes)

》 The following options are here to help you put what you've learned into practice. But if God has prompted you to do something else through this session, then by all means do that!

GROUP ▼

choose 1:

☐ know it

Choose Bible verses that already have meaning for you, and commit them to memory. If memorization isn't easy for you, try these steps:

1. Pray. God says that if we ask for wisdom, he'll give it (James 1:5).
2. Read the passage several times aloud. The more senses you use, the better your memory.
3. Memorize the verse in "chunks"—where it naturally breaks (at commas and periods, for example).
4. Recite the Scripture reference, too. You want to remember *where* the verse is, right?
5. Apply it. Work through the questions we used to explore Joshua 1:1-9. Make Scripture more than just words—make it part of your life.

☐ live it Meditate

for at least five minutes each day on Ephesians 4:21-24. Ask God to show you one thing to "let go"—one thing that you've kept a tight grip on and is keeping you from a fully open and free relationship with God. Also ask God to show you one new thing to "put on"—one thing you can do to live out your new life in Jesus.

☐ share it How has

God's Word spoken to you during tough times? What "ah-ha's" came while reading the Bible that applied directly to that situation? Now think of someone who's going through a similar situation. Guess what! God has already shown you what you can share! So share it. If nothing else, it will show that you care and understand—and that speaks volumes.

Form pairs, select the option you'd like to take on this week, and share your choice with your partner. Write what you plan to do in the space provided, and make plans to connect with your partner before the next session to check in and encourage each other. Take five minutes to do that now.

☐ **go for it** Offer a Bible study to your unchurched friends. You only need a few people for a study like this—maybe even just you and two others. Invite them over, and create an open atmosphere so they feel comfortable. If someone brings up an idea that goes against God's Word, respond openly but without condemnation. Just stick to the facts. People will appreciate both your candor and your acceptance, and through your transparency, they'll catch a glimpse of Jesus.

☐ **do it together**

As a group, commit to a week of spiritual journaling. Write down verses that have become especially meaningful, write prayers to God, record insights—there's no right or wrong way to journal. One of the most important results of journaling comes in looking back at what God has taught you and realizing how far God really has brought you.

...or think of your own!

Because I need God's Word to help me live a transformed life in Jesus, I'll "Walk It Out" by

_____

_____

_____

Walk It Out <small>continued</small>

prayer⊙

Come back together as a group. Ask everyone to hold out their Bibles. As they do, thank God for his Word, and ask him to use it to change your ways of thinking and to help your thoughts and lives become more Christ-like.

Go Deeper

To dig deeper into how to better read and understand the Bible, check out these resources:

God Sightings: The One Year Bible (Tyndale House)

God Sightings: The One Year Companion Guide and *God Sightings: The One Year Small Group Leader Guide* (Group)

Rick Warren's Bible Study Methods: Twelve Ways You Can Unlock God's Word by Rick Warren (Zondervan/HarperCollins)

How to Study Your Bible: The Lasting Rewards of the Inductive Method by Kay Arthur (Harvest House)

Living by the Book: The Art and Science of Reading the Bible by Howard G. Hendricks and William D. Hendricks (Moody)

How to Read the Bible for All Its Worth by Gordon D. Fee and Douglas Stuart (Zondervan)

Tools of the Trade

Just as it would be hard to do carpentry with just a hammer, a saw, or a screwdriver, it's much easier and more productive to study the Bible when you have a variety of tools. Enrich your personal Bible study time with…

- **Bibles**—All right, so you already have a Bible. But having a variety of modern translations—such as the New International Version, New Living Translation, New King James Version, or *The Message*—can also help you see God's eternal truth with a fresh set of eyes. Parallel Bibles are also available; they feature multiple translations side by side. You can find online versions at sites such as biblegateway.com or newlivingtranslation.com.

  There are also a number of excellent study Bibles that are wise investments for any serious student of the Bible. Most study Bibles include features such as study notes, maps, and a concordance. The *NIV Study Bible, Thompson Chain-Reference Bible, Life Application Bible, Discover God Study Bible, Ryrie Study Bible,* and *Nave's Study Bible* are just a few good options. The NET Bible (netbible.org) is also a great online study Bible, with great commentaries to go with it. If you're looking to get into the habit of Bible reading, check out *God Sightings: The One Year Bible.* Or look over topical Bibles, which list verses by topic, or chronological Bibles, which organize Scripture in historical order rather than the usual canonical order and show how the books of the Bible are intertwined. (For example, Paul's letter to the Galatians is followed by the Jerusalem Council discussion about the same issues in Acts 15.)

- **Concordance**—An exhaustive concordance lists nearly every word found in the Bible. Different concordances exist for different translations of the Bible. You can look up other verses that have the same key word in them. Exhaustive concordances also list the original Hebrew, Aramaic, or Greek word used, so you can see if the same original word was translated differently into English. Some good ones are *Cruden's Complete Concordance, Strong's Exhaustive Concordance, Young's Analytical Concordance to the Bible,* and blueletterbible.org.

- **Bible Dictionary**—A Bible dictionary provides an alphabetical listing of biblical terms and names, with information as to their meaning, and also allows you to discover the meaning of many Hebrew and Greek words. Not all words in the Bible are listed in a Bible dictionary (unlike a concordance). *Unger's Bible Dictionary* or Tyndale's *New Bible Dictionary* are two good examples.

- **Encyclopedia of Bible Words**—Similar to a standard encyclopedia, this tool can be used to determine the meanings behind Bible words. However, the encyclopedia does not list strict definitions but short articles about the meanings of the words.

- **Commentaries**—A commentary is one person's or one group's view of the meaning of a passage of Scripture. There are numerous commentaries on the market, ranging from older to more modern. They can be quite helpful in trying to understand the meaning of a text, but keep in mind that a commentary is only one person's take (or representative of only one particular theological view-point). Different commentaries will have different views on what a verse means. It can be beneficial to look at several different commentaries when trying to determine the meaning of a specific Bible passage.

- **Bible Atlas**—Keep a Bible atlas on hand so you can identify locations where most historical events in the Bible took place.

- **Spiritual Journal**—While all the tools mentioned above have the benefit of thousands of hours of scholarly work and study behind them, don't overlook opportunities to record and reflect on those things that God speaks to *you* personally through the Bible and through experiences in your faith walk. See the "Do It Together" suggestion in this session for more ideas on how to use a spiritual journal, or try *God Sightings: The One Year Companion Guide* (Group).

- **Have problems reading, but still want to delve into God's Word?** Have no fear. The electronic media are breaking down this barrier more and more. Listen to podcasts. Download messages from your church's (or other churches') websites. Get an audio Bible (CD or MP3), and play it in your car. Or for more in-depth study that provides visuals, audio files, and movie clips as well as print materials, try a resource such as *iLumina* (Tyndale House).

  Whatever you need, it's probably already out there. May God bless your search, open your mind, and fill your heart even further with his Word!

Worship—It's Not Just Singing

And from the throne came a voice that said, 'Praise our God, all his servants, all who fear him, from the least to the greatest' " (REVELATION 19:5).

In this session, we'll journey...

from ————————————→ **to**
tapping into the ways God has wired each of us for worship...

discovering how worship both honors God and changes us.

Before gathering, make sure you have...

- ○ worshipful music and something to play it on✶

- ○ newsprint tablet, blackboard, or white board (If you're in a small-group setting, a notepad is OK.)

- ○ a special snack or dessert for all to see but not eat right away✶

✶See **Leader Notes**, page 194, for details.

Come and See

(about 10 minutes)

Ask everyone to form pairs and share their answers to these questions:

Allow three minutes for discussion, and then bring everyone back together. Ask for a few volunteers to share their answers before going on to the next question.

Allow a couple of minutes for responses. If no one responds, that's OK—let the silence hang out there before moving on. You'll get another shot at this issue later on.

> *Worship in this life is like one grand rehearsal for the real thing... we do not keep the discipline of worship; worship keeps us.*
>
> —Robert Banks and R. Paul Stevens, The Complete Book of Everyday Christianity

》 Over the last several weeks, we've looked at different ways to respond to and become more connected with God, such as quiet time, prayer, and Bible study. We often call these spiritual disciplines, but all of them are forms of worship—ways to acknowledge that we serve a great God, to recognize God's "worth-ship." They get us out of our own way so we can see and appreciate God for who he is. Our worship declares that God is God—and we aren't. And thank God for that!

As we've looked at these different approaches to worship, you've probably been more naturally drawn toward certain ones than to others. Perhaps you enjoy having quiet time with God, whether that's while reading your Bible, praying, or just being still. Perhaps you've been more drawn to the music or the atmosphere we've created here today. Or maybe you just can't wait for Sunday service so you can let it all out!

Here's the good news: These are all legitimate ways to worship God! And while we should use all of them—and other ways as well—we shouldn't ignore that God has built each of us to connect with him in our own unique way. So let's learn more about how we can worship God the way God has already wired us, and what keeps us from doing that.

Come and See

◎ What activity do you most enjoy doing with a friend?

◎ How does doing that activity together show the other person that he or she is important to you? How does it help you enjoy the activity more?

◎ What do you do to show God that he's important to you?

Seek and Find

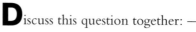

(about 30 minutes)

Discuss this question together: ——————————————

Write down everyone's responses to your first question so all can see them, acknowledging each person's contribution as you do so. Then go on to the next question: ——————————

Write down any new ideas that come up. Then continue: ———

Seek and Find

◎ When you think of worship, what words come to mind?

◎ Out of the answers we gave, which ones do you think most fit God's idea of worship? Are there others we haven't mentioned yet?

◎ Do you normally think of worship more as a shared experience or a personal one? Why?

◎ Can worship be both shared and personal at the same time? Explain (or better yet, give examples).

Seek and Find continued

>> **Let's make this discussion a little more personal now. Form groups of three or four. Let's dig into what we've learned the last few weeks, as well as how you've encountered God in worship elsewhere in your life. Discuss the following questions:** ————

Come back together as a larger group, and share highlights and insights from group discussions.

>> **It's amazing how God meets us where we are and uses what we have and who we are. At the same time, we shouldn't be surprised—God made us the way we are!**

So who's thinking about that [name the snack or dessert] **over there?** (Pause for reactions.)

Hang in there—we're close to wrapping things up. So let's start making our way to the end...

◎ Of the activities we've done over the last few weeks—both inside and outside of this group—which ones have helped you connect with God the most? Why?

◎ Talk about a meaningful time or season of worship—of any kind— you've had in the past. What made it so meaningful to you?

◎ How has your idea of what worship is (and isn't) changed during the course of your Christian life? How has your own worship of God changed as a result?

Go

(about 15 minutes)

》 ...the *very* end. Would someone volunteer to read Revelation 19:5-10?

After your volunteer reads,

》 Put yourself in the middle of this passage. Go from being an observer to being a participant—because that's what you'll be one day. And let's discuss this further. ————————————————————

It's more than a little remarkable to think about, but it's important to remember that our lives are prep time for *eternity.* At this very time in our lives, we're being prepared to live forever in God's presence. Just thinking about that will help us look at our lives differently, so set aside time this week to reflect on the fact that one day we'll be with God forever, worshipping him!

We'll also begin taking a more intentional, hands-on approach to worship this week, not only through the "Walk It Out" activity, but also by exploring how God has specifically wired each of us for worship. At the end of this session is a section called "How Do You Connect With God?" Work through this section this week—it will probably take about 20 to 30 minutes for you to complete—and think about how you can connect more to God in the way he's made you. When you touch base with the person you're paired up with this week, be sure to share what God has shown you as you look at the ways *you* connect with God.

So let's start to "Walk It Out."

> *But you might wish to think about... whether you really would be comfortable for eternity in the presence of One whose company you have not found especially desirable for the few hours and days of your earthly existence.*
>
> —*Dallas Willard,*
> The Great
> Omission

✝ **Revelation 19:5-10**

◎ Does this scene excite you, make you uncomfortable, or does it just not resonate with you? Explain your answer.

◎ Our [dessert/snack] isn't exactly a wedding feast, but you're probably looking forward to enjoying it. How does the anticipation right now affect how much you'll enjoy it later?

◎ By the same token, how does (or should) knowing our eternal future with Jesus help us make worship—*however* we do it—a higher priority in our lives right now?

Walk It Out

(about 5 minutes)

» **The following options are here to help you put what you've learned into practice. But if God has prompted you to do something else through this session, then by all means do that!**

---

choose 1:

live it It can become easy to just go through the motions in our devotional time. Consciously commit to not letting that happen this week. As you start, be quiet before God. Picture God in all his glory. Desire to encounter and worship God with a sense of reverence, awe, and devotion. Reflect on how this affects not only your worship but other parts of your life.

know it If you didn't take on the Psalms after Session 4, try them now. At least read Psalms 1; 19; 23; 104; 136; 139; and 144–150. And don't just read—*meditate* on these Psalms; consider everything God (and the psalmist) is saying. As you complete each Psalm, thank God for who he is, and let these Psalms be a spur to worshipping God more deeply.

share it Take your worship time to another level: Spend an entire day, from the moment you wake until you fall asleep, worshipping God with your thoughts, words, prayers, actions, and attitude. Do every task "as unto him." At some point during your day, share with someone what you're doing, and why. Sharing that you're making God your priority might just help that person do the same.

Form pairs, select the option you'd like to take on this week, and share your choice with your partner. Write what you plan to do in the space provided, and make plans to connect with your partner before the next session to check in and encourage each other. Take five minutes to do that now.

☐ **go for it** How can you worship God—*in public*? If you're musically gifted or don't mind others looking on, invite friends to sing, pray, or worship in a nearby public park with you. Be respectful of other people's personal space, but don't be afraid to show your faith and joy. Some passersby might be put off, sure, but others might be curious about what (or who) makes you tick. Who knows? You might even get some additional participants—or the opportunity to share the Source of your joy.

☐ **do it together** What elements of worship do you not normally participate in at your church? Make a list, choose some of them, and do them with your group. For example, if your church only sings choruses, sing hymns. If your church doesn't use the traditional creeds, recite the Nicene or Apostles' Creed (www.silk.net/RelEd/2creeds.htm) aloud. Read from a lectionary. Pray spontaneously. Whatever you do, do it in a way that's totally fresh yet God-honoring.

...or think of your own!

Because God wants me to draw closer to him in worship, I'll "Walk It Out" by

_____

_____

_____

Walk It Out continued

prayer⊙

Come back together as a group. Gather around your snack or dessert. Bless the food, and thank God for all your other blessings—and for the wonderful eternal future with God that is in store for all of you. Also take a few moments to thank God for bringing your group this far—not only as a group, but as individuals who are growing in Jesus. Ask God to help each of your group members gain a deeper sense of how they can connect with God in every part of their lives.

Then celebrate! You're officially halfway through this season! Congratulations! Take an extra bite and enjoy it!

Go Deeper

To dig deeper into ways to draw closer to God in worship, check out these resources:

Pure Praise: A Heart-Focused Bible Study on Worship by Dwayne Moore (Group)

My Utmost for His Highest by Oswald Chambers (Barbour, et al.)

Sacred Pathways: Discovering Your Soul's Path to God by Gary L. Thomas (Zondervan)

The Practice of the Presence of God by Brother Lawrence (Wilder Publications, et al.)

Celebration of Discipline: The Path to Spiritual Growth by Richard Foster (HarperSanFrancisco)

How Do You Connect With God?

There are many different and acceptable ways to connect with God. We worship God in different ways at different times, but God has designed each of us to connect with him more strongly in some ways than others. Worshipping God the way he's created us honors God and helps us draw strength from him to do the other things he's designed us for as well!

The following questionnaire is adapted from the book *Sacred Pathways: Discovering Your Soul's Path to God* by Gary L. Thomas (Zondervan). Read the following descriptions, and rate each statement that follows from 1 (not me at all) to 5 (oh yeah, that's me). Enter your totals in the lines next to the headings. When you've finished, review your totals and the descriptions that follow; then reflect on how God might want to take you deeper in worship. Enjoy the journey!

Traditionalist ____

Traditionalists are drawn to historical elements of faith—rituals, symbols, sacraments, and sacrifice. They tend to have a disciplined life of faith. Structure, rather than being a hindrance to their faith, keeps them connected to God.

____ The words *tradition, history, symbols,* and *anniversary* are very appealing to me.

____ I enjoy church traditions celebrating Thanksgiving, Advent, Christmas Eve, Lent, Passover, and Easter.

____ I would enjoy reading biographies telling the spiritual secrets of my Christian heroes and how they practiced their faith.

____ I feel closest to God when I'm participating in a familiar form of worship that has memories dating back to my childhood. I am bothered when the church is too contemporary.

____ I feel that individualism within the church is a real danger. Christianity is a corporate faith that needs corporate expression rooted in tradition.

Contemplative ____

Contemplatives seek to love God with the deepest, brightest, most nearly pure love imaginable. The focus is not necessarily on serving God, doing God's will, or accomplishing great things in God's name, but on God himself. Their predominant views of God would be as loving Father or as our Bridegroom.

____ The most difficult times in my faith are when I can't feel God's presence within me.

____ When I think of God, I think of love, friendship, delight, and adoration more than anything else.

____ I would enjoy reading a book titled *Friendship With God*.

____ I feel closest to God when my emotions are awakened, when God quietly touches my heart, tells me that he loves me, and makes me feel like I'm his closest friend.

____ I really enjoy having 30 minutes of uninterrupted time a day to sit in quiet prayer and "hold hands" with God, writing love letters to him and enjoying his presence.

Sensate ____

Sensates want to get lost in the awe, beauty, and majesty of God. They are often drawn to the liturgical and grand. When they worship, they want to be overwhelmed by sights, sounds, and smells. Incense, intricate architecture, classical music, and formal language are all possible routes from God's heart to theirs.

____ I feel closest to God when I'm in a church that allows my senses to come alive—when I can see, smell, hear, and almost taste his majesty.

____ I would really enjoy using drawing exercises or art to improve my prayer life.

____ The words *sensuous, colorful,* and *aromatic* are very appealing to me.

____ I'd have a difficult time worshipping in a church building that is plain and lacks a sense of awe or majesty.

____ Beauty is important to me—I have a difficult time worshipping through second-rate Christian art or music.

Ascetic _____

Take away the outside world, and what's left is an Ascetic. Ascetics want to be alone. They live a fundamentally internal existence and are often uncomfortable with any environment that distracts them from listening to God.

_____ A meaningful worship experience for me could involve spending a whole night in prayer, fasting for one or more days, or giving away something that I had treasured.

_____ The words *silence, solitude, discipline, sacrifice,* and *hardship* are very appealing to me.

_____ Adhering to strict personal goals characterizes my life.

_____ I am bothered by the materialism and "me-ism" I see in America.

_____ I feel closest to God when I am alone in a small room and there is nothing to distract me from focusing on his presence.

Naturalist _____

Naturalists would rather leave the building, put down the book, and go pray beside a river. Naturalists are similar to Contemplatives, except that they are moved by creation as well as by the inner world. Just being outdoors moves them to worship God.

_____ I often am made aware of spiritual truths by observing God's creation on display.

_____ A book called *Nature's Sanctuaries: A Picturebook* would be appealing to me.

_____ I feel closest to God when I'm surrounded by what he has made—the mountains, the forests, or the sea.

_____ If I could escape to a garden to pray, walk through a meadow, or take a trip to the mountains, I would be very happy.

_____ I feel cut off if I have to spend too much time indoors. Nothing makes me feel closer to God than being outside.

Activist _____

Activists serve a God of justice. They define worship as standing against evil and calling sinners to repentance and often view the church as a place to recharge before going back into battle against injustice. They may adopt either social or evangelistic causes and are energized by their interaction with others—even if that interaction is mostly conflict.

____ I would like to awaken the church from its apathy.

____ I feel closest to God when I'm standing up for his justice, writing letters, picketing, or urging people to vote.

____ The book written by Franky Schaeffer, *A Time for Anger*, would be an appealing book for me to read.

____ The phrases *courageous confrontation, social activism,* and *political action* appeal to me.

____ I get very frustrated if I see apathetic Christians who don't become active. I want to drop everything I'm doing and help the church overcome its apathy.

Intellectual ____

Intellectuals live in the world of concepts. They may be shy or withdrawn, and thus might actually avoid intellectual confrontation, but they are still fed primarily by intellectual activity. To the Intellectual, faith is something to be understood as much as it is something to be experienced. They feel closest to God when they first understand something new about him.

____ I feel closest to God when I learn something new about him that I didn't understand before. It's very important to me that I know exactly what I believe.

____ The words *concepts* and *truth* are very appealing to me.

____ I get frustrated when the church focuses too much on feelings and spiritual experience. Of far more importance is the need to understand the Christian faith and have proper doctrine.

____ I spend more money on books than on music.

____ I feel close to God when I participate in several hours of uninterrupted study—reading God's Word or good Christian books and then perhaps having an opportunity to teach or participate in group discussion.

Enthusiast ____

As Sensates want to be surrounded by beauty and Intellectuals want to grapple with concepts, Enthusiasts are inspired by joyful celebration. They don't just want to know God—they want to experience God and his power. If their hearts aren't moved, something's wrong.

____ People would say I am physically expressive in my worship.

____ The words *celebration, joy,* and *excited* appeal to me.

____ I spend more money on music than on books.

____ I feel closest to God when my heart is sent soaring and I feel like I want to burst with joy. Celebrating God and his love is my favorite form of worship.

____ I expect that God is going to move in some unexpected ways.

____ God is an exciting God, and we should be excited about worshipping him. I don't understand how some Christians can say they love God, and then act like they were "weaned on a dill pickle" whenever they walk into church.

Caregiver ____

Caregivers love God by serving others. They see Jesus in the poor and needy, and their faith is built up by interacting with others. Rather than wearing them down, caring for others energizes them.

____ I sense God's power when I am counseling a friend who has lost a job, preparing meals for someone, fixing a computer, or spending a week at an orphanage in Mexico.

____ A book titled *99 Ways to Help Your Neighbor* would be very appealing to me.

____ I grow weary of Christians who spend their time singing songs while a sick neighbor goes without a hot meal or a family in need doesn't get help fixing their car.

____ I feel closest to God when I see him in the needy, the poor, the sick, and the imprisoned. You can count on me to offer to help someone in need.

____ The words *service* and *compassion* are very appealing to me.

For Extra Credit

(OK, so it's not really extra credit, but you'll still learn something important...)

Go back to the "Walk It Out" options for this week. Look them over, and identify which activities go with which worship style. You'll learn something more about yourself, about others in your class and church, and about the body of Christ. God has wired us all differently! *Vive la différence!*

We're in This Together

"Is there any encouragement from belonging to Christ? Any comfort from his love? Any fellowship together in the Spirit? Are your hearts tender and compassionate? Then make me truly happy by agreeing wholeheartedly with each other, loving one another, and working together with one mind and purpose" (PHILIPPIANS 2:1-2).

In this session, we'll journey...

from ————————————→ **to**
exploring how our relationships
with others affect our relationship with Jesus...

identifying ways we can pursue
Jesus together.

Before gathering, make sure you have...

○ a cooler half full of ice cubes✶
○ drinks for everyone✶

Optional activities (choose one or both in Seek and Find):

Option A:
○ "Seek and Find," as is (see page 120)

Option B:
○ DVD of *Finding Nemo* (see page 128)✶

✶See **Leader Notes**, page 196, for details.

Come and See

(about 15 minutes)

Encourage everyone to pour a drink before getting comfortable. Engage in a bit of small talk. Don't jump into the session—take the opportunity to relax first. Once everyone is relaxed, discuss these questions:

》 We often tend to expect something more when we're with other Christians, don't we? In some ways, though, these expectations set us up for a fall. Scripture, in fact, says we *are* fallen people. We're *going to* let each other down. It's inevitable. Without Jesus, we're all lost causes.

The trick, then, is not simply to pursue relationships with other Christians, but to pursue Jesus *together as* Christians. The two things sound similar, but there's all the difference in the world between them. When we make Jesus the focus, suddenly all those little things that often get in the way in our relationships don't seem so important. When we pursue Jesus together, our relationships *naturally* become closer and deeper because we're letting *Jesus* set the tone. And Jesus is never going to steer us the wrong way.

Let's spend some time today exploring how this can become more of a reality in our lives.

> *All the blessings we enjoy are Divine deposits, committed to our trust on this condition, that they should be dispensed for the benefit of our neighbors.*
>
> —John Calvin,
> The Institutes
> of the Christian
> Religion

◎ What is it about just hanging out that helps people loosen up and become comfortable with one another? What else do we do to help lower our guards with each other?

◎ OK, here's one more question: What keeps us from "getting real" with other Christians? Why?

Seek and Find

(about 20 minutes)

If you've chosen **Option A**, *read on.*
If you're doing **Option B**, *go to page 128.*

Ask for a volunteer to read Acts 1:6-11.

》 Let's stop for a few moments and try to picture this: One minute Jesus is right there with his apostles—the people he's entrusted to share his life and message with the rest of the world—and the next, he's gone. And on top of that, two men in white clothing— presumably angels—show up and, in essence, ask, "What are you doing just *standing* there?" Let's talk about this. ─────

Ask for another volunteer to read Acts 1:12-17, 21-26, then discuss: ──────────────────────────────

✝ Acts 1:6-11

◎ How do you think the apostles felt at that moment?

◎ In what ways do you feel (or have you felt) as though you're "just standing there" in your Christian walk, waiting for Jesus to tell you what to do?

✝ Acts 1:12-17, 21-26

◎ How did Jesus' followers respond, once they got past their initial shock?

◎ How does knowing other Christians you can trust and share your struggles with—no matter what kind of struggles they are—help you stop standing still and move forward?

Seek and Find continued

> *It has been said that true friendship begins only when people share a common memory and can say to each other, 'Do you remember?' Each of us is one of a great fellowship of people who share a common experience and a common memory of their Lord.*
>
> —William Barclay,
> The Daily Study
> Bible

Form groups of four or five. Read John 17:20-23 and Ephesians 4:1-6, and discuss: ————————————————

✝ **John 17:20-23; Ephesians 4:1-6**

◎ According to these passages, in what ways do we already have unity as Christians?

◎ Describe a time you tried to go it alone—without being connected with a church or group—whether it was before or since you came to know Jesus. What was that like?

◎ Now describe a time you've experienced God bringing a church or group together for a purpose. What was that like? What was the difference between those two experiences?

◎ Who do you know right now who's not only your friend but who also is someone who pushes you closer to Jesus? Tell us a little about him or her.

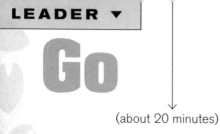

(about 20 minutes)

 》 Everyone go back to the cooler, take one ice cube, and then stand in a circle.

If there are more than 12 people, form groups of six to eight for this experience.

》 Hold hands with the people on each side of you, with the ice between your hands. Hold hands tightly until the ice completely melts. Don't let go. It's going to get cold, but remember, we're all in this together!

When the ice has fully melted, drop hands. Blow on your hands, rub them together, and get your circulation back.

Then read Philippians 2:1-5, and answer these questions: ──────

》 Now find a partner, and discuss this week's "Walk It Out" options. Pray together about the choices you make. When you've finished, you're free to quietly leave [or quietly hang out until everyone's finished, if you're in a small-group setting].

✝ Philippians 2:1-5

◎ What was it like as you held on to the ice—and it got colder? Did it make it better or worse to know that your partners were going through the same thing? Explain.

◎ How does standing together with others help us keep Jesus a priority in our lives, even (or maybe especially) when things are tough?

◎ If you could ask this group for advice or prayer on just one thing right now, what would it be?

◎ Who right now would you really like to develop a spiritual relationship with? Not just a friendship, but a relationship in which Jesus is the important person?

Walk It Out

(about 5 minutes)

>> **The following options are here to help you put what you've learned into practice. But if God has prompted you to do something else through this session, then by all means, do that!**

GROUP ▼

choose 1:

know it

Using a concordance or online keyword search, do a word study on *unity*. Discover what God has to say about how we're already in this together as Christians, and what he wants to do to draw us even closer together. Then ask God what he wants *you* to do.

live it

Encourage other people this week. Share something very specific that will be a real encouragement to them. If you're married, watch for an opportunity to tell your spouse how much you appreciate him or her. If you have children, let them know when they're doing something right—or just what wonderful people you think they are. Let co-workers or neighbors know you're there for them. Then stand by your words.

share it

What do you enjoy doing outside of church or group? Write it down on a sheet of paper. On the other side, list names of other people you'd like to know better. Consider reaching out to at least one of them by inviting him or her to join you in one of the activities you listed. Be sure to build in some time to just talk and develop a deeper relationship with this person.

Form pairs, select the option you'd like to take on this week, and share your choice with your partner. Write what you plan to do in the space provided, and make plans to connect with your partner before the next session to check in and encourage each other. Take five minutes to do that now.

go for it

How can you support someone at your workplace or in your neighborhood with more than just words? Perhaps you know someone who is going through a trial you've gone through yourself. Listen to his or her feelings and experiences—how are they like what you went through, and how are they different? How did God meet you in that situation? What did others do for you that might help this person now? Let the person suggest ways you might help, too. Then follow through.

do it together

Have some fun together this week. No projects— just laughs. What would you all enjoy? Have a party. Do a shared activity. Have a time just worshipping together in song. Whatever you do, have fun—and joy—together.

...or think of your own!

Because I need genuine relationships with other Christians to help me grow in Jesus, I'll "Walk It Out" by

_____

_____

_____

_____

_____

SEEING IT DIFFERENTLY
Seek and Find—Option B

Instead of the original "Seek and Find," try it this way. You'll be watching two scenes from *Finding Nemo*. For the first scene, cue the movie to 0:25:11 (DVD Chapter 9), when Nemo is thrown into the fish tank. Stop the clip at 0:27:59, at "I'll go deflate him…" Then discuss these questions: ————————————

Ask for volunteers to read John 17:20-23 and Ephesians 4:1-6, and discuss these questions: ————————————

Now watch another scene from *Finding Nemo*. Cue the movie to 0:28:58 (still DVD Chapter 9, but a little past where you stopped in part 1), where Nemo is swimming up to the picture of Darla. Stop the clip at 0:30:31, at "I'm Nemo." Then discuss the following questions: ————————————

Pick up at "Go," which begins on page 124.

◎ What things in this clip remind you of the first time you walked into a church or when you first encountered another group of Christians? If you're a lifelong Christian, what first impression do you think your church or group would make on someone who doesn't know Jesus?

◎ When have you committed some of the mistakes the fish made?

◎ When have you felt as Nemo did in this clip—wishing other Christians could see past their own quirks, habits, and routines and simply be there for *you*? Explain.

 **John 17:20-23; Ephesians 4:1-6**

◎ According to these passages, in what ways do we already have unity as Christians?

◎ Describe a time you tried to go it alone—without being connected with a church or group—whether it was before or since you came to know Jesus. What was that like?

◎ How did Gill's scars and imperfections help him help Nemo? How did that help Nemo be truly accepted by the other fish?

◎ When has someone who's been through the same trials really been there for you (or when have your trials helped you help someone else)?

◎ Who do you know right now who's not only your friend but who also is someone who pushes you closer to Jesus? Tell us a little about him or her.

Go Deeper

Here are more great resources to dig deeper into the importance of Christian community:

Making Room for Life: Trading Chaotic Lifestyles for Connected Relationships by Randy Frazee (Zondervan)

Organic Church: Growing Faith Where Life Happens by Neil Cole (Jossey-Bass)

Creating Community: Five Keys to Building a Small Group Culture by Andy Stanley and Bill Willits (Multnomah)

Life Together: The Classic Exploration of Faith in Community by Dietrich Bonhoeffer (HarperOne)

The Holy Spirit and You

Therefore, dear brothers and sisters, you have no obligation to do what your sinful nature urges you to do. For if you live by its dictates, you will die. But if through the power of the Spirit you put to death the deeds of your sinful nature, you will live. For all who are led by the Spirit of God are children of God" (ROMANS 8:12-14).

In this session, we'll journey...

from ————————————→ **to**
exploring how the Holy Spirit works *in* our lives...

discovering how the Spirit can work *through* our lives each day.

Before gathering, make sure you have...

○ a platter of assorted fruit✱

○ a bunch of grapes✱ (Make sure there's at least 1 grape for each person.)

○ newsprint tablet, blackboard, or white board (If you're in a small-group setting, a notepad is OK.)

✱See **Leader Notes**, page 197, for details.

Come and See

(about 20 minutes)

》 **Welcome. Today's session is on the Holy Spirit—and where there's the Spirit, there's fruit! So I hope you've enjoyed some of that fruit already. We'll get to the grapes later—I promise. For now, let's jump in and look at that "fruit of the Spirit" passage. It's found within Galatians 5:16-25.**

Ask for a volunteer to read Galatians 5:16-25.

》 **Let's read one more quote—it's on your group page. Go ahead and read it to yourselves.** ——————

Allow 30 seconds for everyone to read. Then form groups of three or four to discuss the following questions: ——————

Allow five minutes; then come back together to share highlights and insights from small-group discussions.

Pass around the bunch of grapes, and let everyone take at least one grape. Ask people to take a few moments to look at their grapes and then hold them up so everyone else can get a look at them, too.

> *It is interesting that the Bible talks of the fruit of the Spirit rather than the fruits. A tree may bear many apples, but all come from the same tree. In the same way, the Holy Spirit is the source of all fruit in our lives.*
>
> —*Billy Graham*

◎ Do you agree with this quote? disagree? something in between? Explain.

 Galatians 5:16-25

◎ Regardless of your answer, which of the fruit (or fruits) listed in Galatians do you think are most evident in your life right now? Which ones could use a little more fertilizer? Why?

Come and See continued

>> Some grapes are riper, some are smaller, some may even be a bit discolored, but they're all grapes, and they all came from the same source. They didn't grow by themselves, and they didn't grow completely apart from one another. The same is true of us. As Christians, we all belong to Jesus, and whatever spiritual growth we have—whether it's individually, as a group, or as the church—comes from being connected to the Spirit of God.

Go ahead and eat your grapes now, and let's discuss these questions: ——————————————

Write down everyone's answers to the second question for all to see. Make a point of acknowledging each person's contribution as you do so.

>> The Bible says the Spirit is already within those who believe in Jesus (Romans 8:9). Since that's true, you'd think it would be pretty easy to connect and live life in the Spirit in all these ways we've just listed, right?

But a lot of times, we can still feel disconnected from the Spirit—like we're going through the motions and we're not sure whether we're really living life in the Spirit. And sometimes—let's be honest—we choose not to listen to what the Spirit is trying to tell us. Many times, though, we're just not very good at recognizing when the Spirit is trying to guide us. We haven't properly trained our "spiritual ears," so to speak, to listen for the Spirit. That's where we're starting today.

Come and See

◎ How does living by the Spirit help us produce the fruit of the Spirit?

◎ Practically speaking, what does it mean for us to live by the Spirit? What does that actually look like? Let's list some ideas.

GROWING IN JESUS / SESSION 9   135

Seek and Find

(about 25 minutes)

Discuss these questions: ───────────────────

Assign one of the passages below to each member of your group. Ask people to form pairs.

- John 14:25-26
- John 16:7-14
- Acts 1:4-8
- Romans 8:26-27

- 1 Corinthians 2:9-15
- 2 Corinthians 3:7-9, 16-18
- Galatians 4:6-7
- Ephesians 1:13-14

》 In your pairs, read your passage to yourself. Then take turns showing your partner what your passage says about the Spirit. But don't just explain it—act it out, raise your voice, move around, do whatever it takes to fully convey the meaning. Be persuasive, convicting, transforming—whatever this passage says the Spirit does, try to emulate it.

On that note, put some room between pairs because it could get loud in here!

Allow about five minutes for pairs to do their dramatic readings. Regroup, and have each pair share insights from the passages they read. Then discuss these questions: ───────

◎ How would you explain to a friend *who* the Holy Spirit is and *what* the Spirit does?

◎ What would you like someone to explain to *you* about the Spirit?

✝ John 14:25-26; John 16:7-14; Acts 1:4-8; Romans 8:26-27; 1 Corinthians 2:9-15; 2 Corinthians 3:7-9, 16-18; Galatians 4:6-7; Ephesians 1:13-14

◎ Out of these attributes of the Spirit, which ones have you seen at work in your own life? Which ones are new or still kind of hard for you to grasp? Explain.

◎ All acting aside, how might other people help us understand how (or when) the Spirit is trying to guide us?

◎ On the other hand, how might others get in the way of us hearing what the Spirit is trying to tell us?

◎ How can we better train our "spiritual ears" so we really know whether it's the Spirit who's trying to guide us? How could you do this in your own life?

(about 10 minutes)

Ask for a volunteer to read Galatians 3:2–5.

》 This is a tough passage, but let's start on the positive side. ————————————————————————

Most congregations of professing Christians today are saturated with a kind of dead goodness, an ethical respectability which has its motivational roots in the flesh rather than in the... Holy Spirit.

—Richard F. Lovelace, **Dynamics of Spiritual Life**

After your discussion, go to "Walk It Out" on page 140.

✝ Galatians 3:2-5

◎ Was there a time in your life that you can think back to and say, "Yeah, the Spirit *had* to have been in that"? What was that like?

◎ Read verse 3 again. How have you seen this to be true in the church today?

◎ Let's take that to another level: How do you take—or how have you taken—things out of the Spirit's hands in your own life? Why do you think you've done it?

◎ What's one way you need to trust God's Spirit to work and bear fruit in your life? How can we, as a group, help you do that?

Walk It Out

(about 5 minutes)

》 **The following options are here to help you put what you've learned into practice. But if God has prompted you to do something else through this session, then by all means do that!**

choose 1:

☐ know it

Get to know more about the Spirit's role in your life and in the life of your church. There are several Scripture passages in this session to help you get started. You could also read Romans 8 or look up passages about the gifts of the Spirit such as Ephesians 4 or 1 Corinthians 12. Don't stop at reading, though— spend some time asking God to open your mind and heart to what the Spirit wants to do in your life.

☐ live it

Take time each day to ask yourself, Have I displayed the fruit of the Spirit in my actions and attitudes? Is there any pruning God needs to do in my life? If so, what would it look like? Also consider keeping a journal this week to help you reflect on how the Spirit is working through your circumstances and guiding you through them.

☐ share it

Think about how the power of God's Spirit has already changed your life. How can you share that with someone else? What might the Spirit's power look like in that person's life? Commit to calling that person this week and setting up a time to meet.

Form pairs, select the option you'd like to take on this week, and share your choice with your partner. Write what you plan to do in the space provided, and make plans to connect with your partner before the next session to check in and encourage each other. Take five minutes to do that now.

☐ go for it
Go out for coffee or pizza with a couple of friends this week. Are they struggling with issues that the power of the Spirit could help them with? Have they ever even considered turning to God for help? Be creative! Read Romans 8:6-11, and challenge them to take God at his word. Share how God's power has made a difference in your own life. Or share something from this session. The point is to get your friends to start asking themselves important questions.

☐ do it together
Who are the powerless in your community, those who really need to see God's power and love? Together, identify one such group. Ask God how he wants you to get involved and how the Spirit could shine through your actions. Consider your passions, your availability, and your location. Work together to identify a practical, meaningful way you can help, and then get to it!

...or think of your own!

Because I want to allow the Spirit to work through my life every day, I'll "Walk It Out" by

_____

_____

_____

Walk It Out continued

prayer⊙

Come back together as a group, and listen to one another's prayer requests. As an introduction to your prayer time, read Galatians 5:22-23 again; then pray that the fruit of the Spirit would be evident in each person's life, as the Spirit guides and works through each situation you're praying for. If enough grapes are left, let everyone take another grape and hold it during the prayer as a reminder of the connection your group has through the Spirit.

Go Deeper

To dig deeper into what it means to live in the Spirit, here are some great resources:

Gospel Transformation (World Harvest Mission)

Fresh Wind, Fresh Fire: What Happens When God's Spirit Invades the Hearts of His People by Jim Cymbala (Zondervan)

The Divine Embrace: Recovering the Passionate Spiritual Life by Robert E. Webber (Baker)

Dynamics of Spiritual Life: An Evangelical Theology of Renewal by Richard F. Lovelace (InterVarsity)

The Spiritual Man by Watchman Nee (Living Stream Ministry)

The Battle of Your Life

For we are not fighting against flesh-and-blood enemies, but against evil rulers and authorities of the unseen world, against mighty powers in this dark world, and against evil spirits in the heavenly places" (EPHESIANS 6:12).

In this session, we'll journey...

from ⟶ **to**
recognizing that all Christians have a spiritual enemy... | identifying how the Spirit helps us to fight the *spirit*ual battles we face.

Before gathering, make sure you have...

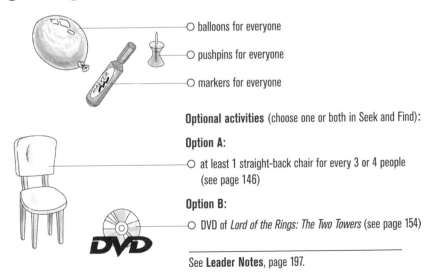

- ○ balloons for everyone
- ○ pushpins for everyone
- ○ markers for everyone

Optional activities (choose one or both in Seek and Find):

Option A:
- ○ at least 1 straight-back chair for every 3 or 4 people (see page 146)

Option B:
- ○ DVD of *Lord of the Rings: The Two Towers* (see page 154)

See **Leader Notes**, page 197.

Come and See

(about 10 minutes)

》 **Welcome back! Last week we discovered how we let the Holy Spirit work through our lives. This week we're going to look at other spiritual matters—but not the same spirit. Form groups of four, and discuss these questions:** ──────────

Allow five minutes for discussion; then bring everyone back together, and ask for volunteers to share highlights from their small-group discussions.

》 **This week we're going to consider another, better-known bully: Satan. A lot of people have different ideas of who the devil is—or *if* he even is. But the Bible assures us that Satan is very real and that he's determined to oppose us, whether we acknowledge it or not.**

More important, we're assured that even though we're in a battle, Jesus wins. More than that, the Bible shows us how we can live in that victory more and more each day. Let's discover how.

> *My dear brothers, never forget, when you hear the progress of enlightenment vaunted, that the devil's best trick is to persuade you that he doesn't exist!*
>
> —Charles Baudelaire, "Le Joueur généreux"

◎ Were you ever picked on or harassed by a bully? If so, share a little about that experience. What things did you do to keep the bully from bothering you? How successful were you?

◎ What advice would you give your own children about dealing with a bully?

Seek and Find

(about 30 minutes)

Ask for a volunteer to read Ephesians 6:10-13. Then discuss this question: ──────────

If you've chosen **Option A**, *read on.*
If you're doing **Option B**, *go to page 154.*

》 Get back into your foursomes. Make sure each group has at least one straight-back chair. Have one person sit, and have at least one person stand on each side of him or her. Those standing will push gently against the seated person's arms, while the person who is sitting will try to raise his or her arms straight out to the side. Those of you standing—do your best to make sure that doesn't happen.

Take about 30 seconds for each person to try to raise his or her arms, and then switch. Make sure everyone gets a turn.

As soon as you are washed in Christ's blood and clothed in His righteousness, you must begin to hew your way through a lane of enemies, right up to the eternal throne. Every foot of the way will be disputed; not an inch will Satan yield to you.

—Charles Spurgeon

Allow about two minutes for everyone to have a turn; then ask groups to discuss these questions: ──────────

Allow 10 minutes for discussion, and then call everyone together to share highlights and insights from the small-group discussions.

✝ **Ephesians 6:10-13**

◎ What's your reaction to Paul's statement that we are fighting against mighty powers in this dark world and against evil spirits in the heavenly places (verse 12)? Does it make you frightened and insecure? challenged and really pumped? skeptical? something else? Explain.

◎ How much success did you have raising your arms? How could we have bent the rules to make it easier?

◎ When have you felt a heaviness or pull upon you that you knew wasn't just about you—whether you'd call it temptation, a spiritual battle, an addiction, or whatever? What have you learned from those struggles?

◎ Did (or do) you ever consider taking a "shortcut" or doing something that's "less than God's will" to lessen the pain of those kinds of experiences? Explain.

◎ What makes it so hard to fight through these kinds of battles? What helps you stay focused on God and his desires for you during those times?

Seek and Find continued

>> **Let's move from looking at the reality of spiritual warfare to the tactics. How does Satan actually go about trying to mess us up? And how should we respond? Let's start by looking at two of the best-known "Satan stories" in the Bible.**

Ask for volunteers to read Genesis 3:1–6 and Luke 4:1–13. Then discuss:

✝ **Genesis 3:1-6; Luke 4:1-13**

◎ How are these two accounts similar? How are they different?

◎ Look at the strategies Satan uses in each of these passages. How do you see these same kinds of strategies used today? What do they look like?

◎ Why is it sometimes easier for us to believe the lies of Satan rather than Jesus' promises? What can we do to counter that?

Go

(about 5 minutes)

Give everyone a balloon, and have a variety of markers available. Let people blow up their balloons and tie them.

》 **Think of one way that you *know* Jesus has changed the way you see yourself. It might be that you see yourself as totally forgiven, as God's child, or as someone Jesus really cares about. Write or draw this on your balloon. Make it as simple or creative as you like!**

Give people a minute or two to write or draw on their balloons, and then ask them to rejoin their smaller groups one more time.

Give everyone a pushpin.

》 **I think you know what's going to happen next.**

The youngest person in your group will go first. That person will turn to the person on the right and pop that person's balloon. Give yourselves a few moments to react between each popping. Go around your group until everyone's balloon has been popped.

After everyone's balloon has been popped, discuss: ————————

Come back together, and share highlights from the discussions.

Ask for a volunteer to read Ephesians 6:14–18, and then answer these questions: ————————————————

》 **Find a partner and read the "Walk It Out" options together. Once you've decided what you each want to do, take another minute to share your answers to this last question we've discussed. In what ways is Satan "popping your balloon" right now? In what ways do you need the Spirit to step in and help you through this issue? Share your thoughts with your partner. Then pray for each other. When you've finished, you're free to quietly leave** [or quietly hang out until everyone's finished, if you're in a small-group setting].

> *The story of your life is the story of the long and brutal assault on your heart by the one who knows what you could be and fears it.*
>
> —John Eldredge, Waking the Dead

◎ How did it feel to have your own balloon popped? to pop someone else's balloon?

◎ What are some ways the devil or forces of evil try to "pop your balloon" and keep you from being the person you know you are in Jesus?

✝ **Ephesians 6:14-18**

◎ Paul refers to several spiritual weapons here. Which of these weapons do you rely on the most? How? Which of these spiritual weapons could you use an "upgrade" in?

◎ Now that we've looked at where each of us is most susceptible to attack and where our defenses are weakest, what's one thing you can do to more effectively fight your spiritual battles?

Walk It Out

(about 5 minutes)

>> **The following options are here to help you put what you've learned into practice. But if God has prompted you to do something else through this session, then by all means, do that!**

choose 1:

□ know it

Use your "sword" every day (Ephesians 6:17). If you're not already reading your Bible regularly, commit to a goal of reading at least 10 minutes each day. If you're already reading your Bible regularly, increase your goal. Let your sword sharpen *you* this week.

□ live it

Where have you been most susceptible to attack? Sexual temptation? Addiction? The need for "stuff"? Commit to avoiding situations where temptation is most likely and to praying for that area of your life daily. Also find someone who will hold you accountable in that area. You might be sitting with him or her right now!

□ share it

Who do you know who seems to be under a great deal of spiritual pressure? Maybe he or she is facing some kind of harassment, encountering more than the usual amount of temptation, or simply going through a very difficult time. Be sensitive to ways you can support this person, such as sending a note of encouragement or personally intervening on his or her behalf—whether that's with God or with other people.

Form pairs, select the option you'd like to take on this week, and share your choice with your partner. Write what you plan to do in the space provided, and make plans to connect with your partner before the next session to check in and encourage each other. Take five minutes to do that now.

☐ **go for it** Follow Jesus' humble example by doing a modern-day act of service for a friend. If your friend compliments you for your good deed, simply thank that person for his or her kind words, and leave it at that. But don't discount any compliment by downplaying your abilities or how God has moved you to use those abilities—it can be an act of humility to accept praise from another person, too.

☐ **do it together**
There are people all around the world who are in some sort of bondage to sin, whether by choice or not. Address one of those needs together. Volunteer to help at a crisis-pregnancy center, to help mothers overcome their bondage to guilt and fear. Or raise funds and supplies for a group such as Justice for Children International (jfci.org), which works toward the elimination of child exploitation and sex trafficking. Check your hearts; then let God move you forward.

...or think of your own!

Because spiritual warfare is upon me whether I acknowledge it or not, I'll "Walk It Out" by

_____

_____

_____

SEEING IT DIFFERENTLY
Seek and Find—Option B

LEADER   Instead of the chair activity, watch a scene from *Lord of the Rings: The Two Towers*. Cue the movie to 1:05:53 (DVD Chapter 17), when Gandalf turns around. Stop the clip at 1:08:26, after Gandalf says, "I fear for the survival of Rohan."

GROUP

◎ What reasons does Theoden give for not fighting? Do you think they're good reasons or just excuses? Explain.

◎ What do you think of Aragorn's statement, "Open war is upon you, whether you would risk it or not"? Do you really believe you're already in a spiritual battle? Why or why not?

◎ What makes it so hard to fight through these kinds of battles? What helps you stay focused on God and his desires for you during those times?

Pick up at the leader statement, **Let's move from looking at the reality of spiritual warfare to the tactics**, on page 148.

Go Deeper

To dig deeper into understanding spiritual warfare and how to fight the spiritual battles that will come, here are some great resources:

Battlefield of the Mind: Winning the Battle in Your Mind by Joyce Meyer (FaithWords)

The Bondage Breaker by Neil T. Anderson (Harvest House)

The Holy War by John Bunyan (NuVision Publications)

Spiritual Warfare in a Believer's Life by Charles H. Spurgeon (Emerald)

Overcoming Sin and Temptation by John Owen (Crossway)

Seeing Others as Jesus Does

" *If you give special attention and a good seat to the rich person, but you say to the poor one, 'You can stand over there, or else sit on the floor'—well, doesn't this discrimination show that your judgments are guided by evil motives?"* (JAMES 2:3-4)

In this session, we'll journey...

from ————————————→ **to**
recognizing our inclination to judge others...

discovering how to change so that we love others as Jesus would.

Before gathering, make sure you have...

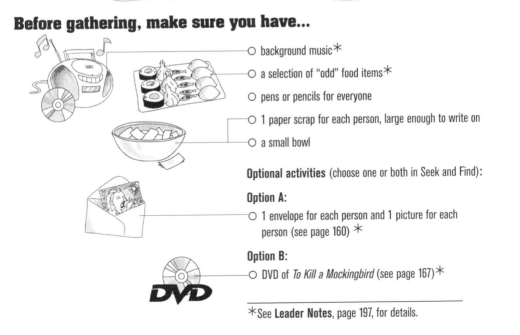

○ background music ✶
○ a selection of "odd" food items ✶
○ pens or pencils for everyone
○ 1 paper scrap for each person, large enough to write on
○ a small bowl

Optional activities (choose one or both in Seek and Find):

Option A:
○ 1 envelope for each person and 1 picture for each person (see page 160) ✶

Option B:
○ DVD of *To Kill a Mockingbird* (see page 167) ✶

✶See **Leader Notes**, page 197, for details.

Come and See

(about 10 minutes)

Call people together before they've had a chance to help themselves to the snacks you've provided.

》 **We have a special assortment of snacks today. Take whatever you like—and leave whatever you don't!**

Give everyone a few minutes to load up their plates (or turn up their noses!). While people taste the snacks, discuss these questions:

》 **It's easy to like people who like us or people we have things in common with. And let's face it: It's hard to like someone who, intentionally or not, has done something to offend us or who seems to put up barriers between us.**

The thing is, Jesus doesn't just call us to be there for the people we like. We need to remember that God met each of us in our weaknesses and our faults, and if he can change us, he can change anyone. So let's move forward and try to expand our field of vision so we can better see others the way Jesus sees them.

◎ Are there any foods here that made you say to yourself, I'm not trying *that*? Are you reconsidering your decision, after watching others eat it? Why or why not?

◎ By the way, what do you think of the music? How come?

◎ Think about a time your first impressions of someone turned out to be totally wrong (in a good way). What initially "turned you off" to that person? What happened to change your perspective?

Seek and Find

(about 30 minutes)

If you've chosen **Option A**, *read on.*
If you're doing **Option B**, *go to page 167.*

Pass out the envelopes you've prepared. Let everyone open their envelopes, and then discuss these questions: ————————

> *A basic temptation: the flatly unchristian refusal to love those whom we consider, for some reason or other, unworthy of love. And on top of that, to consider others unworthy of love for even very trivial reasons.*
>
> —Thomas Merton, Conjectures of a Guilty Bystander

Form groups of three or four. Ask for a volunteer to read James 2:1-9.

❯❯ **Think about the reactions you've had so far to music, to food, and now to people you don't even know (and maybe even to each other's reactions!). Now let's discuss these questions:** ————————

Call everyone back together to share highlights or questions from small-group discussions.

❯❯ **Let's jump a little further ahead in James, to Chapter 4. Will someone volunteer to read verse 1 and then jump to verses 4 through 12?**

> Prejudice: *A hostile opinion about some person or class of persons. Prejudice is socially learned and is usually grounded in misconception, misunderstanding, and inflexible generalizations.*
>
> —The New Dictionary of Cultural Literacy, Third Edition, 2002

Let your volunteer read James 4:1, 4-12.

❯❯ **Last week we looked at the subject of spiritual warfare and how we're already involved in spiritual battles whether we acknowledge them or not. Sometimes it's easier to focus on the battle going on "out there," but let's bring this closer to home and discuss these questions:** ————————

◎ What's your initial reaction to the picture in your envelope? Would you invite this person to dinner if you had the chance? Why or why not?

◎ Why is it so easy for us to judge people we don't even know?

◎ On the other hand, how do we play favorites with those who are more popular or influential, even when we don't like them?

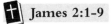 **James 2:1-9**

◎ How are these reactions like the reactions we first have to people who are different from us?

◎ What are some things that aren't necessarily sinful but nonetheless give you a negative impression of people? What do those things reveal about some of our own wrong motives?

✝ **James 4:1, 4-12**

◎ What's the connection between submitting to God so the devil will flee and judging others?

◎ How have you seen this kind of warfare in your own life? How do you deal with it now?

Give everyone a scrap of paper and a pen or pencil.

》 Think about a time you felt unfairly rejected or judged by others—for *whatever* reason. On your paper, write a word or phrase that describes how that experience felt. Keep it simple. Then fold the paper.

Ask everyone to place the folded papers in a bowl. Then pass the bowl around, and let each person take one of the folded papers, making sure people don't take their own.

Have people read their papers aloud, and then discuss these questions:

Read 1 Corinthians 1:25-31, and then answer these questions: —

◎ What was harder—writing what you wrote or having it read aloud? Why?

◎ What do these words tell you about how it feels when other people are unfairly judged?

1 Corinthians 1:25-31

◎ How does this passage help put things in perspective—in terms of how God sees you as well as how you should see others?

◎ What can you do to train yourself to see past appearances to see others the way Jesus does?

Walk It Out

(about 5 minutes)

》 The following options are here to help you put what you've learned into practice. But if God has prompted you to do something else through this session, then by all means do that!

choose 1:

know it

The book of James has a lot more to say about our attitudes and actions toward others. So read all of it this week. At five chapters, you can read a chapter each weekday. After each chapter, ask God how he wants you to put what you've learned into practice. Chances are you'll have a lot to work with (and that's OK)!

live it

What barriers come between you and others? Figure out what *your* barrier is, and then deal with it this week. For instance, if you hate cigarette-smoking, join co-workers during their smoking break. (You don't have to smoke, of course; just love the people who do.) Or listen to a political talk show that you normally avoid. Humanize the people who don't share your views, and think about how you can love them.

share it

Who worships in a Christian tradition that's entirely different from yours? Reach out to this person over coffee or lunch, and ask questions. Take time to learn this person's story and traditions. Don't debate differences; look for ways you both connect with God.

Form pairs, select the option you'd like to take on this week, and share your choice with your partner. Write what you plan to do in the space provided, and make plans to connect with your partner before the next session to check in and encourage each other. Take five minutes to do that now.

☐ **go for it** Befriend a neighbor who doesn't belong to your social or economic class, religion, or race. Don't make a mission out of it—just get to know the person. Afterward, reflect on the experience. How did your perceptions change? How will it change the way you approach your neighbors (and others you feel are somehow different from you) in the future?

☐ **do it together**

Neighbors aren't always people you know! So this week, as a group, find some new neighbors. They may be the elderly people at the grocery store who need help getting groceries to the car, the poor or homeless in your town, or those teenagers in your neighborhood who clearly are looking for something better to do. Give them something better: the love of Jesus.

...or think of your own!

Because I need to see others the way Jesus does, I'll "Walk It Out" by

_____

_____

_____

_____

_____

Walk It Out continued

Call everyone together.

>> **Let's take this one step further. This session may have stirred up memories that make you realize that someone's judgment has hurt you more deeply than you'd thought. Or perhaps you've discovered that you haven't really forgiven someone for judging you. You might have a new understanding of how your own judgments have hurt others. Let's take a couple of minutes to reflect silently about these things, and then we'll close in prayer. If there's something you want to ask God's help for out loud, though, please don't be afraid to do so. We won't judge you.**

After at least a minute of silence, pray something like this:

prayer⊙

>> **Lord, your Word tells us, "Do not condemn others, or it will all come back against you"** (Luke 6:37). **And we want to obey you. But we've all been guilty of judging others at one time or another. We don't want to be defined by—or in bondage to—who or what we like or don't like, or by what we're for or against. We want to be defined by *you*. Forgive us for judging others unfairly, and help us see them through your eyes. Help us also to forgive those who have judged us without ever really knowing us, or who haven't forgiven us for what we've done to them, and to approach those people as you would.**

Allow a few moments of silence so others have the opportunity to add their prayers if they want to; then close.

>> **Lord, open our eyes so that we can really see others, and *love* others, the way you've called us to—the way you already love us. In Jesus' name, amen.**

SEEING IT DIFFERENTLY

Seek and Find—Option B

LEADER Instead of the envelope activity and the discussions that follow it, try this: Watch a scene from *To Kill a Mockingbird*. Cue the movie to 0:8:52 (DVD Chapter 4), when Jem says, "There goes the meanest man who ever took a breath of life." Stop the clip at 0:10:27, when Jem says, "I was just tryin' to warn him about Boo, but he wouldn't believe me." Then discuss these questions:

GROUP

◉ How much of this story do you believe? How much do you think is made up?

◉ Would you have wanted to meet Boo Radley after hearing all this? Why or why not?

Ask for a volunteer to read James 2:1-13, and then discuss these questions:

GROUP

 James 2:1-13

◉ Why is it so easy for us to judge people we don't really know?

◉ What are some things that aren't necessarily sinful but nonetheless give you a bad impression of others? What do those things reveal about some of our own wrong motives?

Resume the session with the discussion of James 4 beginning on page 160.

To dig deeper into how to better see others through "God glasses," here are some great resources:

God Space: Where Spiritual Conversations Happen Naturally by Doug Pollock (Group)

The Emotionally Healthy Church by Peter Scazzero, with Warren Bird (Zondervan)

Humility by Andrew Murray (Wilder Publications, et al.)

Churches That Heal: Becoming a Church That Mends Broken Hearts and Restores Shattered Lives by Doug Murren (Howard Books)

Why Do Christians Shoot Their Wounded? Helping (Not Hurting) Those With Emotional Difficulties by Dwight L. Carlson (InterVarsity)

Sharing Your Life in Jesus

No one lights a lamp and then puts it under a basket. Instead, a lamp is placed on a stand, where it gives light to everyone in the house. In the same way, let your good deeds shine out for all to see, so that everyone will praise your heavenly Father" (MATTHEW 5:15-16).

In this session, we'll journey...

from ⟶ **to**

identifying how we've already encountered Jesus personally...

learning how to share our life in Jesus with others, no matter who they are.

Before gathering, make sure you have...

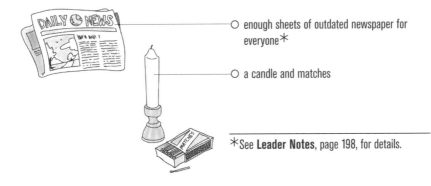

○ enough sheets of outdated newspaper for everyone ✳

○ a candle and matches

✳See **Leader Notes**, page 198, for details.

Come and See

(about 15 minutes)

Have everyone find a partner and discuss this question: ——

Allow five minutes for discussion. Call everyone together, and ask for a few volunteers to share highlights from their discussions.

"The greatest temptation that assails Christians is that in effect, for most of us, the Gospel has ceased to be news. And if it is not news it is not Gospel: for the Gospel is the proclamation of something absolutely new...Any word that comes from God is news!"

—Thomas Merton,
Conjectures of a
Guilty Bystander

Pass out the sheets of outdated newspaper to everyone, and allow about 30 seconds for people to look them over. Then discuss these questions: ——————————

》 It's been said that we may be the only gospel some people ever read. If our own sense of what Jesus has done for us—and is doing in our lives *right now*—is like the paper each of us is holding, it's easy to understand why no one is buying it.

What would help us treat the gospel of Jesus Christ as if it were still "breaking news"—for us and for others? That's what we're going to explore today.

◎ When have you been an eyewitness to a big event? How did being there and seeing it for yourself affect you? affect how you talked about it to others?

◎ Do you recall any of the stories you see here? Do any of them appear to be relevant to your life right now? Why or why not?

◎ What's a "big story" you remember that now makes you wonder how you got so worked up over it? How did you (and others) respond to it at the time?

◎ The word *gospel* means "good news"—in fact, the gospel of Jesus Christ is the best news of all. Do we still treat it like news or more like…well, like these old newspapers? Why?

Seek and Find

(about 30 minutes)

》 **I'm going to read 1 John 1:1-4. Everyone else, simply close your eyes and listen. Each time I pause, think about what was just read, and imagine what John and his readers must have actually experienced as they read or relived what's being described in this letter.**

Read 1 John 1:1-4, pausing for five seconds each time you come across a sensory word, such as *heard, seen,* or *touched.*

》 **Now form groups of four, and discuss these questions:** ——————————

Call everyone back together to share any highlights or questions from the small-group discussions. ——————

Turn off the lights in your meeting area (make sure you've read the next question to yourself before you do it!). Have your own answer to this question ready, in case no one else wants to share:

Turn the lights back on. Ask for a volunteer to read Matthew 5:14-16; then discuss these questions: ——————

> *Preach the Gospel at all times and when necessary use words.*
> —St. Francis of Assisi

> *Better to light a candle than to curse the darkness.*
> —Chinese proverb

✝ 1 John 1:1-4

◎ Why is it important for us today to know that John and the other disciples heard and saw and touched Jesus?

◎ Discuss a time you were able to share your own experience with Jesus with someone else, or when someone else observed your faith and responded to it in some way. How did sharing your faith affect that person? How did his or her responses affect you?

◎ Tell about a time you felt in the dark and disconnected from Jesus—even if you were already a Christian. What happened to "turn the light on" for you?

✝ Matthew 5:14-16

◎ What was it like to have the lights turned back on?

◎ Keeping your own reactions in mind, why might some people prefer living in darkness to coming into Jesus' light?

◎ Do you think some people *need* a spotlight on them to "get it" when it comes to Jesus? Explain.

◎ How can we help people's eyes adjust to the light of Jesus? What do we need to change in ourselves so we can help others see that light?

(about 10 minutes)

>> During the past half-hour, you've had the opportunity to share some examples of ways Jesus has made himself visible in your lives and how he's used that to let your faith shine before others. While we're already being candid about how we let our faith shine, let's keep being transparent with this next question as well: ————

Ask for a volunteer to read 1 John 1:5-9; then discuss these questions: ————

◎ Be honest: What holds you back from letting your light shine more than it does right now?

✝ **1 John 1:5-9**

◎ How can being honest about our sins and flaws actually help others see Jesus more clearly? How have you seen this to be true in your own life?

◎ What could help you live out your life in Jesus more openly—so that both the people you care about and those you don't even know can see it?

Walk It Out

(about 5 minutes)

》 **The following options are here to help you put what you've learned into practice. But if God has prompted you to do something else through this session, then by all means do that!**

choose 1:

live it Practice your listening skills this week. Don't do it with a motive in mind, just do it because you want to build relationships. Listen to others' stories, ask questions about their lives, and actively listen as they talk. Pray for them as the opportunity arises.

know it
Read the entire book of 1 John, one chapter per weekday. Each day, write down your answers to these two questions: "What does this passage say?" and "How do I need to change because of what I've read?" Share your daily record with your partner in the upcoming week.

share it Share with a not-yet-Christian friend one way in which your relationship with Jesus has changed your life. Remember that when light first comes to someone in darkness, it can be uncomfortable and may be met with resistance. Don't be pushy; simply be open about how Jesus has changed your life.

Form pairs, select the option you'd like to take on this week, and share your choice with your partner. Write what you plan to do in the space provided, and make plans to connect with your partner before the next session to check in and encourage each other. Take five minutes to do that now.

☐ go for it *and* do it together

Hold a social event as a group, inviting not-yet-Christian friends and family members. Plan something fun, such as a cookout, Super Bowl party, game night, or holiday celebration. Use this time to build meaningful relationships and show genuine love. Consider specific ways you can reflect Christ's hope to the people you meet in the coming weeks.

...or think of your own!

Because I need to share my life in Jesus with others more fully, I'll "Walk It Out" by

_____

_____

_____

_____

_____

_____

Walk It Out continued

prayer⊙

Call everyone together. Turn the lights off one more time, and light a candle. Encourage group members to confess how they've hidden the light of Jesus from others, and ask God to help you to have the courage and wisdom to truly "let your good deeds shine out for all to see, so that everyone will praise your heavenly Father."

Go Deeper

To dig deeper into ways to genuinely share your faith in Jesus, here are some great resources:

God Space: Where Spiritual Conversations Happen Naturally by Doug Pollock (Group)

Outreach Ministry in the 21st Century: The Encyclopedia of Practical Ideas (Group)

Becoming a Contagious Christian by Bill Hybels and Mark Mittelberg (Zondervan)

Outflow: Outward-Focused Living in a Self-Focused World by Steve Sjogren and Dave Ping (Group)

Organic Church: Growing Faith Where Life Happens by Neil Cole (Jossey-Bass)

The Externally Focused Church by Rick Rusaw and Eric Swanson (Group)

Evangelism Outside the Box: New Ways to Help People Experience the Good News by Rick Richardson (InterVarsity)

What Now?

Therefore, since we are surrounded by such a huge crowd of witnesses to the life of faith, let us strip off every weight that slows us down, especially the sin that so easily trips us up. And let us run with endurance the race God has set before us" (HEBREWS 12:1).

In this session, we'll journey...

from ⟶ **to**
reflecting on where God has taken you over this past season... | identifying where God wants to take you from here.

Before gathering, make sure you have...

○ a pen or (preferably) pencil for everyone (There's a good chance people will want to make corrections as they go along!)

○ a loaf of crusty bread for every 10 to 12 people—large enough so everyone in the group gets a piece

See **Leader Notes**, page 198, for details.

Come and See

(about 10 minutes)

》 So here we are—the end of this season. Today our focus will be twofold. We're going to look back at the journey God has taken us on these past few months—and as we do that, we'll also consider the next steps God wants us to take.

Let's start by spending a few minutes reflecting on the journey God has already taken us on together. ——

Come and See

◎ What expectations did you have when you started this season, if any? How did your actual experience compare to your expectations?

◎ What would you say the most memorable moment of this season has been?

Seek and Find

(about 25 minutes)

》 **Let's take what you've just shared and break it down further. While we're at it, let's bring Jesus' own words into the process.**

Ask for one or more volunteers to read John 15:1–17. Then discuss these questions: ————————————————————

》 **Let's take this one step further.**

Form groups of three or four. Individually, and as a group, you're going to reflect on what God has been showing you over this past season and where you think God may be leading you next. There won't be a "Walk It Out" section this week. That's because you're going to spend the rest of this session working out your commitment–not for just this coming week, but also well beyond.

✝ **John 15:1-17**

◎ How have you felt more connected to Jesus—and to other Christians—over the past few months? (Don't restrict your answer to your experiences just within this group.)

◎ How have you felt God pruning you over the last few months? What's been the fruit of that process so far?

◎ What's one way you need to remain in Jesus, in a way you really haven't until now?

Seek and Find continued

>> On your Group page is a "Personal Mission Statement," which you're going to work through in your groups. Don't approach it with the idea that you have to get everything just right. You're a work in progress, and God knows that— because he's the one who's working in you. But capture as best you can what God has been doing in your life and what you sense God is leading you to do in response to that.

Hopefully the questions we've discussed so far have already started you thinking along these lines. Here are three more that may give you additional help:

- How have you felt most challenged by this study?

- What's the one most important thing you've learned (or rediscovered)?

- Since God has impressed you with this, what do you think God wants you to do about it?

Write your responses on your sheet. You don't have to fill out every section, but if God has been speaking to you, take time now to respond and put that commitment into writing.

When you've finished, share your answers with the rest of your group. Then together, discuss this question:

- Over the past few months, how have you seen God working through the other people you're sitting with?

If the responses to this question inspire you to add to what's already on your sheet, add it now!

OK, go ahead and have at it in your groups. You'll get about 15 minutes. If you finish early, use your extra time to pray for one another.

Allow 15 minutes for people to write and discuss their responses, and then bring everyone back together.

Personal Mission Statement

The most important thing God has shown me through this study is…

_____

_____

_____

_____

_____

In response to what God has shown me and to how God has worked
in my life during this study, I'll respond to God's challenge…

personally by

_____

_____

_____

in my relationships by

_____

_____

_____

_____

in my world by

_____

_____

_____

_____

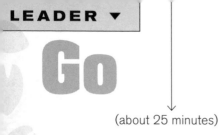

Go

(about 25 minutes)

Ask for a volunteer to read Hebrews 12:1-3. Then discuss: ─────

Bring out the loaf of bread, and ask people to form a circle. (No hand-holding necessary! But if you want to, that's OK, too.) If you have a large group, form circles of 10 to 12 people, and give each group a loaf.

》 **We've shared a lot these past few months—our lives, our struggles, and most important, the grace that God has shown each of *us* through Jesus. So let's take one more opportunity to remember this before we all move forward.**

When the loaf of bread is passed to you, tear off a piece; then pass the loaf to the person on your right. As you pass it, thank God for the person you're passing it to. Thank God for what that person has brought to this group. Be as general or specific—or as quiet—as you're comfortable being.

After everyone has had a chance to share and pray, give permission for everyone to eat their piece of bread. As they do, close your time in prayer.

prayer⊙

》 **Lord, thank you for the people here, what they've brought to this group, how you've been working inside and through each of them, and your plans for each of them. Put people in our paths who will help keep us on your path—to encourage us, to stick with us when we're struggling, to help us work through what you're trying to do in our lives. Help each of us to be that person for others as well—in this group, in your church, and in each person you've created. In Jesus' name, amen.**

Hebrews 12:1-3

◎ How have you seen some of the things you've learned about during this season modeled by others? How has it inspired you to keep running the race (or to really *start* running it)? Be specific.

◎ How can members of this group support you as you take the next steps God is calling you to take?

For those wanting to dig deeper into discovering God's plan for their lives, here are some great resources:

The Purpose-Driven Life: What on Earth Am I Here For? by Rick Warren (Zondervan)

Holy Discontent: Fueling the Fire That Ignites Personal Vision by Bill Hybels (Zondervan)

Visioneering: God's Blueprint for Developing and Maintaining Vision by Andy Stanley (Multnomah)

General Tips

- **Read ahead.** Although these sessions are designed to require minimum preparation, read each one ahead of time. Highlight the questions you feel are especially important for your group to spend time on.

- **Preview DVD clips.** The copyright doctrine of fair use permits certain uses of very brief excerpts from copyrighted materials for not-for-profit-teaching purposes without permission. If you have specific questions about your intended use of copyrighted materials, consult your church's legal counsel. Your church can obtain a blanket licensing agreement from Christian Video Licensing International for an annual fee. Visit cvli.com, or call 888-771-2854 for informaton.

- **Enlist others.** Don't be afraid to ask for volunteers. Who knows? They may want to commit to a role such as teaching a session or bringing snacks once they've tried it. However, give people the option to say "No, thanks" as well.

- **Be prompt.** Always start on time. If you do this from the beginning, you'll avoid the tendency of group members to arrive later and later as the season goes on.

- **Gather supplies.** Make sure to have the supplies for each session on hand. (All supplies are listed on the opening page of each session.) Feel free to ask other people to help furnish supplies. This will give them even more ownership of the session.

- **Discuss child care.** If you're leading a small group, discuss how to handle child care—not only because it can be a sensitive subject but also because discussing options will give your group an opportunity to work together *as* a group.

- **Pray anytime.** Be ready and willing to pray at times other than the closing time. Start each session with prayer—let everyone know they're getting "down to business." Be open to other times when prayer is appropriate, such as when someone answers a question and ends up expressing pain or grief over a situation he or she's currently struggling with. Don't save it for the end—stop and pray right there and then.

- **Let others talk.** Try not to have the first or last word on every question (or even most of them). Give everyone an opportunity to participate. At the same time, don't put anyone on the spot—remind people that they can pass on any questions they're not comfortable answering.

- **Stay on track.** There are suggested time limits for each section. Encourage good discussion, but don't be afraid to "rope 'em back in."

- **Hold people accountable.** Don't let your group off the hook with the assignments in the "Walk It Out" section— this is when group members apply in a personal way what they've learned. Encourage group members to follow through on their assignments.

- **Encourage group challenges.** Also note that "Do It Together"—the last weekly challenge in "Walk It Out"—is meant to be done as a group. Make sure that group members who take on these challenges are both encouraged and organized.

- **Pray.** Finally, research has shown that the single most important thing a leader can do for a group is to spend time in prayer for group members. So why not take a minute and pray for your group right now?

Session 1

- Review the General Tips beginning on page 189.

- If this is the first time you're meeting as a group, take a few minutes before your session to agree on a few simple ground rules. Here are three important ones:

  1. Don't say anything that will embarrass anyone or violate someone's trust.

  2. Likewise, anything shared in the group *stays* in the group, unless the person sharing it says otherwise.

  3. No one has to answer a question he or she is uncomfortable answering.

- Being able to grow as a Christian is often dependent on being confident in one's own relationship with Jesus. If some group members are still unsure whether they have a personal relationship with Jesus, direct them to passages such as Romans 10:9-10 and Ephesians 2:8-9. Sometimes it's as easy as showing people what *God* says, rather than what they believe about themselves.

  But in other cases, the issue goes deeper than that. If either you or they still have doubts, set aside time when you can talk one-on-one, or promptly refer them to your pastor or another Christian leader you trust.

- Give group members extra encouragement not only to write their faith stories but also to find someone to share them with. In our field test, one participant used this as an opportunity to share his faith story with a not-yet-Christian friend. This opened the door to many more discussions with that person.

- At the conclusion of this first session, make a special point to remind group members of the importance of following through on the weekly challenge each has committed to in the "Walk It Out" section.

Session 2

- If new people join the group at this time, use part of the "Come and See" time to introduce them to the group, and have people pass around their books to record contact information (page 22). Give a brief summary of the points covered in Session 1.

- Review the supplies list. For Option A, the older and smellier your "old, beat-up coat" is, the better—but it shouldn't be so bad that people would get dirty just putting it on! (Know any mechanics or landscapers who'd loan you their coats for the day?) Pair up your old and new coats, and put your pairs where everyone can easily access them.

- On that note: If there are not-yet-Christians in your group, the idea of throwing off an old life and putting on a new life in Jesus may be totally foreign. Be prepared to explain this concept if you need to, but don't preach it. Doing this activity may even offer an opportunity to get together with this person or persons during the next week, to answer questions they might have and open them up further to receiving that new life in Jesus.

- You'll notice that we put people in pairs to share their faith stories. Be sure to do this, rather than doing it as a group. It will give people more time to share and will feel less threatening.

- For your closing prayer time, consider asking for volunteers to pray for requests that were shared. You could also minimize the time you spend sharing prayer requests by just diving into praying. Don't tell each other about the requests; just tell God, and let others listen. If certain requests need to be explained later on, spend some time afterward discussing those requests so people know how to pray during the week for one another.

Session 3

- Review this week's supplies list. You might consider offering lactose-free options in addition to milk, if you know that certain group members have allergies. Also, try to offer homemade cookies. Store-bought will work in a pinch, but the good stuff will be even more effective.

- In our field test, our host made sure the cookies were fresh out of the oven when the group arrived. Remember, the more senses you engage, the better a session sticks.

- Are you praying for your group members regularly? It's the most important thing a leader can do for his or her group. Take some time now to pray for your group, if you haven't already.

Session 4

- Now that you're a month into this season, you may find it helpful to make some notes right after your session to help you evaluate how things are going. Ask yourself, Did everyone participate? and Is there anyone I need to make a special effort to follow up with before the next session?

Session 5

- Remember the importance of starting and ending on time, and, if necessary, remind your group of it, too.

- If you need to spend more time than just one week on a given session—and if you're not tied to a calendar and *can* spend some extra time—then *do it!* Taking the time to understand what God wants to tell your class, group, or accountability partner(s) is way more important than "covering the material."

  If you anticipate this session would be such an opportunity—and it was when we field-tested it—we'd recommend not simply stopping in the middle. Do "Seek and Find" as its own session, and do the other pieces either before or after. (We did "Seek and Find" first, but I suspect that doing it later could be even more powerful. And it was very powerful the way we did it—those three questions alone elicited enough deep discussion to last an entire evening.)

Session 6

- This would be a good time to remind group members of the importance of following through on the weekly challenges they've committed to in "Walk It Out"

- Note that the opening activity requires enough room for everyone to stand at least an arm's length apart. If you meet in a small room, think of how you can briefly expand or relocate your meeting area for this activity.

- Likewise, for the closing activity, we ask that everyone has a wallet, purse, or cell phone handy. These items don't have to be out for the entire session—just make sure they're not in another room if that's where they're normally kept so they're easy to get.

  Also, as you ask that question about the Bible being "joined to your hip," go ahead and slap the place where you keep your own cell phone, wallet, or purse, for emphasis.

Session 7

- Congratulations! You're halfway through this season. It's time for a checkup: How's the group doing? What's worked well so far? What might you consider changing as you approach the remaining sessions?

- Review the supplies list. The style of music is your call—a praise CD, a Bach cantata, a Phil Keaggy instrumental collection, a Messiaen chamber piece, a Gregorian chant... whatever you think will work. But make sure it works as background music rather than foreground music, and play it softly as your group members enter the room. Here are a couple other environmental changes we'd suggest for this session (and any other sessions for which you think they'd be appropriate):

1. Light candles (unscented or lightly scented, for the sake of those with allergies). Dim the regular lighting as much as possible in order to create a contemplative atmosphere while still allowing people to see around the room.

2. If there are other physical elements specific to the way your church does its services, consider including some of those as well.

- If you're not the greatest cook, enlist someone's help in preparing the snack or dessert. Remember, it should be special! Place the dessert or snack where it will be visible (and smell-able) to everyone. If people ask, let them know it's for later. This created *huge* anticipation in our field test.

- Don't explain to the group why your setting is different this week—let them make their own observations and mental connections as the session progresses.

- If a group member has a musical gift, let him or her use it and lead everyone in song for the first 10 minutes or so. I know, I know; worship isn't *just* singing, but singing is certainly one way to worship—and one that could make this session extra-special. After our field-test team worshipped together on this occasion, worship became a regular and special part of our time together.

  Also, be sure to keep the songs God-focused because, honestly, a lot of what passes for worship music these days isn't. Here are a few suggestions: "How Great Is Our God," "How Great Thou Art," "Take My Life," "God of Wonders." You probably have your own ideas; use them. And take joy in God's presence as you do!

- After asking the question "When you think of worship, what words come to mind?" write down everyone's responses, no matter how "off" they may seem at first. Encourage answers that express what people actually feel or think during worship time (whether it's "joy," "a sense of God's presence," "boredom," or "too much hugging") as well as more obvious answers such as "singing," "praise," "prayer," or "silence."

Session 8

- Review the supplies list. Offer whatever cold drinks are appropriate to your meeting time—juice, soft drinks, milk—your call. Try to have diet options, too. If you'd like to supply other snacks, that's fine; just make sure you have a cooler full of drinks ready.

- If your class or group normally has some social time before class, switch things up this week. Tell everyone you're going to start the session right away and socialize afterward. You might get some quizzical looks and comments (we certainly did during the field test), but you'll also be setting up your session perfectly.

- Near the end of "Seek and Find," there might be dead silence after the question, "Who do you know right now who's not only your friend but who also is someone who pushes you closer to Jesus?" At the very least (and this was more our experience during field-testing), there'll probably be a lot of "hmmm"s. Either way, it's OK. This is a *huge* question that people need to answer, if they haven't already.

- An average-size ice cube takes five to seven minutes to completely melt, so do something to make the time go faster during the ice-cube activity. Sing a song, tell stories about the coldest you've ever been, or just exaggerate your whining about how your hands are going numb. (By the way, in our field test this was the activity that convinced the game-hating curmudgeon I mentioned in the Introduction of the value of experiential learning. From this point on, he not only enjoyed the study but the experiences as well!)

Session 9

- Have you been spending time in prayer for the group? If you haven't already, do that right now.

- Before people arrive, have the fruit platter set out, and encourage them to take from it as they come in. However, don't let anyone take grapes until after you've started your session. (Place an "Off Limits" sign in front of the grapes if necessary!) Once you do pass around the grapes, don't be surprised if someone makes a connection to sharing in the Lord's Supper.

Session 10

- Now is a good time to do another group checkup—especially if you're planning on doing another season together after this one. Ask yourself, Is everyone participating? and Is there anyone I need to make a special effort to follow up with?

- Next week's session will require a little preparation by both you and your group members, so go ahead and read the Leader Notes now.

Session 11

- Review the supplies list. For the background music, don't play anything offensive or annoying. However, if the group will look at you funny because of your choice, you're on the right track. Make sure your music is already playing as people enter. Don't quite make it foreground music, but make sure it's loud enough for people to notice it.

- Likewise, concerning the selection of "odd" food items: Ask the group to help supply these things, and ask beforehand what each person is bringing. Better yet, ask each person individually so no one knows that others are in on this. Have at least one especially strange food item, and be sure to have enough of each snack for everyone to sample.

- For the "Seek and Find" activity, include pictures of famous or notorious people everyone would recognize, as well as a few people from other cultures or of a different social standing than your group. Place a picture in each envelope before your session.

- For extra impact, show up in a style of clothing that's "not you"—preferably of a social group you suspect your group wouldn't look upon favorably. Again, be tasteful but pointed in your choices if you choose to do this.

Session 12

To order copies of *Season 2: Growing in Character,* visit your local Christian bookstore or group.com.

- For the opening activity, make sure the newspaper is dated enough that there's not much actual "news" in it. A week-old newspaper might be old enough—and could make the point of this activity that much stronger.

- Try to make your meeting area as dark as possible when suggested in the session. The darkened environment can be both calming and powerful. In our field test, one couple talked frankly about the extended time they'd felt "in the dark," which was still ongoing at the time. But because they were able to "bring their stuff into the light," they've experienced a lot of growth since then.

- Since your next session will be the last one of this season, you'll probably want to start discussing what to do after you've completed this study. Will you go on to Season 2? "pull over" and study another subject in more depth? break up and head to different classes? Make your plans now.

Session 13

- Since this is your group's last session in this season, make sure you have a plan for next week and beyond.

- For extra impact, consider having the Lord's Supper together instead of doing the "Go" activity in which the bread is used. It could be a powerful moment for your group. During our field test, just passing around the bread, with its suggestion of the Lord's Supper, worked well. One person said the guy next to him had "made our group time worthwhile every week." Until then, that person had no idea he was having such a positive effect!

Also, have a plan for celebrating your time together. Do something special after your gathering time, or plan a separate celebration for another time and place. Your call.

Here's one more idea: Instead of going right into your next study, spend another week further exploring your Personal Mission Statements. What are your next steps, both individually and as a group? How are you going to respond to God's challenges? Wrestle with those ideas; then spend an extended time in prayer. You can do this during your celebration time or devote a completely separate session to this time of exploration and prayer. However you do it, let God lead!

No matter what you do—congratulations! You've made it through Season 1! I hope God has blessed your walk together these past few months, and that you'll continue to let him lead all of you forward.